Award-Winning

QUILTS

& Their Makers

Vol. II: The Best of American Quilter's Society Shows
1988-1989

Edited by Victoria Faoro

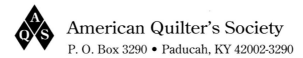
American Quilter's Society
P. O. Box 3290 • Paducah, KY 42002-3290

Additional copies of this book may be ordered from: American Quilter's Society
P.O. Box 3290, Paducah, KY 42002-3290 @$24.95. Add $1.00 for postage & handling.
Copyright: 1992, American Quilter's Society.
This book or any part thereof may not be reproduced without the
written consent of the Publisher.
10 9 8 7 6 5 4 3 2 1

Printed by IMAGE GRAPHICS, INC., Paducah, Kentucky

ACKNOWLEDGMENTS

AQS thanks all of the quiltmakers for giving graciously of their time to respond to questions, for furnishing photographs of themselves and for giving permission to include photographs of their quilts.

AQS also thanks all members of AQS and everyone participating in AQS Shows – those who have entered quilts, volunteered, attended. Without you, the show and this book would not be possible.

AQS also thanks quiltmakers everywhere, who continue to produce the exciting work that first made us want to become involved.

TABLE OF CONTENTS

INTRODUCTION

In 1984 Meredith and Bill Schroeder launched a drive to build an organization dedicated to promoting the accomplishments of today's quiltmaker. Their goals were to develop a membership organization, publish a quarterly magazine for members, hold a national quilt show with meaningful monetary awards, and build a national museum to honor today's quiltmaker.

The American Quilter's Society was the result, along with its magazine *American Quilter*, its annual Quilt Show and Contest, and the new Museum of the American Quilter's Society.

Award-Winning Quilts & Their Makers, Vol. I: The Best of American Quilter's Society Shows, 1985-1987 was published in 1991 to document the first three years of this international show, and the outstanding quiltmakers included.

This book, Volume II, continues this documentation and celebration of quilters and quiltmaking. AQS re-contacted each award winner in the 1988 and 1989 AQS Shows, requesting permission to feature the winning quilt and its maker, and asking for the individual's current thoughts on the quilt, the award it won, and on quilting and competitions in general. The richness of the responses has enabled us to produce a very exciting publication.

AQS is proud to once again present this outstanding collection of quilts and quiltmakers – and looks forward to future volumes. A special thanks goes to quiltmakers and quilt lovers around the world who continue to make each AQS show an exciting event.

Quilt Show & Contest

1988

The fourth American Quilter's Society Quilt Show & Contest was held April 21 through 24, 1988, at the Executive Inn Riverfront in Paducah, Kentucky.

Judges for the quilt show were Chris Wolf Edmonds, Lawrence, KS; Judy Mathieson, Woodland Hills, CA; Katy Christopherson, Lexington, KY.

Category award sponsors were as follows:

Best of Show, American Quilter's Society
Gingher Award for Workmanship, Gingher, Inc.
First Quilt Award, American Quilter's Society
Traditional Pieced, Amateur, Hobbs Bonded Fibers

Traditional Pieced, Professional, Coats & Clark
Innovative Pieced, Amateur, Fairfield Processing Corp.
Innovative Pieced, Professional, Elna, Inc.
Applique, Amateur, V.I.P. Fabrics
Applique, Professional, Mountain Mist
Other Techniques, Amateur, Ameritex
Other Techniques, Professional, Viking/White
Theme: Baskets, Amateur/Professional, That Patchwork Place
Group/Team, Amateur/Professional, Swiss-Metrosene, Inc.
Best Wall Quilt, American Quilter's Society
Wall Quilt, Amateur, Silver Dollar City
Wall Quilt, Professional, Fiskars
Viewer's Choice, American Quilter's Society

In each category three awards were made: 1st place, $800; 2nd place, $550; 3rd place, $300. The Gingher Award for Excellence of Workmanship was a $2,500 award; the Best of Show Award, $10,000; the Best Wall Quilt Award, $2,500; and the First Quilt Award, $500.

The exhibit included 400 quilts representing 48 states, and Canada, Germany, Switzerland, and the United Kingdom. Viewers attending were asked to select their favorite quilt, and a Viewer's Choice Award was made after the show.

A block contest was also held during the show, along with the second quilted fashion contest sponsored by Hobbs Bonded Fibers, and even more activities were available throughout the city of Paducah.

Jane Blair
Conshohocken, Pennsylvania

Gypsy In My Soul

A professional quilt artist and quiltmaking teacher, Jane Blair specializes in new design possibilities from traditional pattern beginnings. In this award-winning quilt, the Queen Charlotte's Crown block was used in the medallion center as well as the double border, with added squares and applique. Jane comments: "The appliqued vines help to make the geometric shapes into a floral statement." She adds, "The blocks are difficult to find because they are not colored in the traditional way.

best of show

1988 AQS Show & Contest

Unusual color and placement of the traditional are characteristic of my work." She hopes her quilts help people understand the degree to which "color can change the ordinary."

Constructed of cottons and cotton/polyesters, this quilt is hand pieced, hand appliqued and hand quilted. Jane comments, "Hand sewing is comforting and relaxing for me. I use machine work only in the binding or when it is absolutely necessary." About her quilting she adds, "My quilting plan is rarely organized. Using a hoop, I work from the center out, mark freehand as I go, and quilt wherever I think it looks best."

Jane's quilts have been included in many shows and exhibitions, including Quilt National, and have appeared

in books and television programs. But, she comments: "I always feel whatever I do could be better. I feel the same about GYPSY IN MY SOUL now as when I made it; I was shocked to think it could win top honors because I can see its imperfections so clearly. Although I'm still amazed at its status, I have accepted the fact of that one shining moment."

About making quilts and winning awards, Jane comments: "Although much appreciated, the awards are not necessary to keep me going. I'd make quilts anyway – win or lose. It's a joy to win big prize money and I'll sell quilts to those who'll pay, but quilts are less a business and more a creative need. I make quilts because it's my means of self-expression. There are no hidden motives. I need no other reason. It's what I do."

To other quiltmakers, Jane says: "Just keep 'doing your thing,' whatever that may be. Someday, somewhere, when you least expect it, someone will agree with you."

*"Winning the Best of Show Award has made me sort of a celebrity –
a member of a small group who have won 'THE' prize.
Although honored to be in that group, the expectations of
performance that go along with it are sometimes overwhelming."*

GYPSY IN MY
SOUL
66" x 84"
©1988
Jane Blair

Museum of AQS Collection

9

Julia Overton Needham
Knoxville, Tennessee

Lavender Blue

Julia Overton Needham says of LAVENDER BLUE, "When the quilt was finished I was satisfied with it, but had grave doubts that it would receive the approval of judges. I'm still amazed that it has done so well – it is such a simple design, with limited colors and a very common sashing."

gingher award

for workmanship
1988 AQS Show & Contest

Its applique block pattern is original, "drawn to coordinate with the Garden Maze setting." Julia comments: "I tried to make the applique extend the X that formed at the intersection of the sashing." Constructed of cottons and cotton blends, the quilt is hand pieced, hand appliqued and hand quilted. Julia adds that the "materials were impulse buys over a long period of time. All quilting was devised to follow pattern lines and fill available space."

About LAVENDER BLUE, Julia says, "It was a joy to make, and I could never part with it. Everything seemed to fall into place. This seldom occurs for me. Most times I have several 'hits and misses' per quilt."

Winning this award has given Julia "encouragement to make more quilts." She continues, "If you ask any Gingher Award winner, I think she would say her quilting life has changed. Everyone has new respect for your abilities. It's a pleasant surprise that so many people recognize you. I've received many complimentary letters

and made many new friends through the American Quilter's Society shows."

Speaking of her background, Julia says, "I have been married for 44 years to a retired engineer who likes to attend quilt shows as much as I do. We have two grown daughters, and most of our spare time is spent on our respective hobbies – quilting and woodworking."

To other quiltmakers, Julia says: "Most quilters love to attend quilt shows, so I decided early on I was obligated to share my quilts so we could have more shows to attend. No quilt entries – no quilt shows – that's frightening!" Julia continues, "It's a risk every time you send one off, but isn't everything in life a risk? It's still a thrill just to have a quilt hanging in a show, whether it wins a ribbon or not. Having someone enjoy your accomplishments is reward enough. Every show I've attended, I've seen something to admire in every quilt."

"The sashing material I used in LAVENDER BLUE had been described by several of my guild friends as the ugliest fabric they'd ever seen. That served as the impetus for my proving the purchase had been justified."

LAVENDER
BLUE
72" x 90"
1986
Julia Overton
Needham

Dorothy Arendt
Hedrick, Iowa

Drunkard's Path

For this award-winning quilt, Dorothy Arendt "used the Drunkard's Path pattern from Mountain Mist™." She explains, "Having made two quilts from this pattern and enjoyed them so much, I decided I should make another to have one for each of my grandchildren."

first place

1988 AQS Show & Contest Traditional Pieced, Ama

She says of her background, "I have been married fifty-six years, and we have one daughter, three grandchildren, and one great-grandson. I have made my quilts for my daughter and my grandchildren, as keepsakes. I enjoy making applique quilts most, and my favorite part of quiltmaking is the final step of working with the quilting stitch."

In DRUNKARD'S PATH, Dorothy combined an off-white cotton blend with a navy blue pin-dot cotton fabric. Using her 18" hoop, she quilted a nine-inch feather in each white area, and a border

of the feather pattern.

The quilt has won several blue ribbon awards, including this one and first place at the Iowa State Fair. Dorothy says of the American Quilter's Society award, "Entering the AQS competition and winning the award has given me more confidence and pride in my quiltmaking and helped me gain recognition among other quiltmakers. I have had the pleasure of making many new friends." Dorothy adds: "I was very thrilled with the award and honor I received at the AQS show and banquet."

To other quilters, Dorothy says: "Always strive for accuracy and neatness in all steps of quiltmaking. If you have accomplished these essential requirements and skill, feel confident in entering your quilt in competition."

"I felt DRUNKARD'S PATH was 'just another quilt' when I had it finished. However, after winning several awards, I cherished it highly. I was very happy to present it to my oldest grandson and his wife as a wedding gift."

DRUNKARD'S
PATH
83" x 103"
1987
Dorothy
Arendt

Lucy Burtschi Grady
Albuquerque, New Mexico

Grandmother's Engagement Ring

"I started this quilt," says Lucy Burtschi Grady, "after I had been at the AIQA Show in Houston, when Stearns and Foster were sponsoring contests giving away cruises. I had had a quilt in the first contest – it received an honorable mention for innovative use of fabric." Lucy continues, "I started another quilt thinking I would enter again.

second place

1988 AQS Show & Contest Traditional Pieced, Ama

At one point, my husband said, 'I don't want to go on a cruise, and I think that quilt is too pretty for you to lose it by winning.' " Lucy agreed. She now adds, "Boy, that is confidence, when you think you might win." Lucy normally doesn't enter contests. This quilt was not entered in Houston, and was finished up right after that contest.

Lucy used a Stearns and Foster pattern for her quilt, but adds, "I did use different fabrics. I like to play around with fabrics, to see what I can do with them, to do

something different." The quilt was pieced on the sewing machine, but the applique was done by hand. Lucy explains, "I always hand quilt and use a large frame that my husband made me. I have it up in the middle of the livingroom when I quilt."

Commenting on the construction of the quilt, Lucy says, "People think this would be a hard pattern to make, but it really isn't. The pattern was given, but if you also set it down on graph paper it's really easy to plan and make. I work with graph paper all of the time." Lucy adds, "I am more interested

in the planning of a pattern than the quilting."

Asked if she feels any differently about the quilt now than when she completed it, Lucy says, "Yes, because it was a winner. I liked the quilt when I was working on it, but after I finish a quilt I usually don't like it. I have to put it away for six months and then I like it."

Lucy's mother, aunts, and grandmother were all quilters, but she didn't really start herself until 1976. She made a bicentennial quilt that year because all her friends were making them. Her youngest daughter was in college at that time, so she had more time. Lucy says that she and her sister, Jane Burtschi Hodge of Indianapolis, travel around and show family quilts. Lucy adds, "After I was a winner, I was always asked to also bring that quilt."

Lucy feels that people value her quilts more now. She comments, "After you're a winner, people pay more attention to your quilts. Recently a woman recognized me as the maker of this quilt and hugged me, saying,

"I married into a family where the grandmother was a quilter on a farm in Texas. I think my husband understands me because he used to see his grandmother and aunt working on quilts. He has to put up with a lot."

GRAND-
MOTHER'S
ENGAGEMENT
RING
79" x 96"
1986
Lucy Burtschi
Grady

'I want to hug a person who has won in Paducah!' "

To others, Lucy says, "I think you should make something that you are really interested in and enthusiastic about. Whether you think you will enter it in competition or not, make it because you like it. Then enter it if you want. Just entering is good; winning is great."

Barbara Barr
Buena Vista, Colorado

Jones Pass

Barbara Barr says, "JONES PASS represents the marriage of two of my greatest loves: quilting and our great mountain wilderness." She drafted all the patterns for this quilt herself, except for the center block of tulips which was from Judy Martin's *Scrap Quilts*. She explains, "The Morning Glory block is Judy Martin's adaptation, and the rosebuds are similar to Joyce Schlotzhauer's Curved Two-patch."

third place

*1988 AQS Show & Contest
Traditional Pieced, Ama*

The quilt is constructed of 100% cotton scraps, though Barbara confesses she did have to buy the three shades of green for the background. The quilt is completely machine pieced and hand quilted. Barbara adds, "Each flower has its own quilting pattern. For example,

the morning glories are on a quilted brick wall, the rosebuds on a quilted trellis."

About her background, Barbara comments, "I have been sewing and doing handwork nearly all my life, but didn't make my first quilt until about 18 years ago. By profession I am an active sportswear (ski, bike, golf) designer and pattern maker. For recreation I love to hike and climb the beautiful

Rocky Mountains, which are right outside my door! I've been lucky enough to have had the same husband, Ben, for 36 years, and two daughters for almost that long!"

Barbara says that winning this award has enhanced her life to some degree: "It's wonderful when I meet someone and they actually recognize my name – or remember JONES PASS from the American Quilter's Society Show or from the cover of *Quilter's Newsletter* magazine. Everyone should have moments of glory – JONES PASS provided one of mine."

To other quiltmakers, Barbara suggests: "Don't start out trying to win a contest. I feel you must design a quilt for yourself and make it for your own pleasure. If, when you're finished, you feel it's good enough, go ahead and enter it. Competition is a great learning process. The judges' critiques can be very helpful in improving your skills."

"I knew JONES PASS was special from the beginning, but to have it confirmed by experts makes it even more special. It was on a bed after I finished it, but after it won a ribbon I hung it on the wall!"

JONES PASS
82" x 92"
©1987
Barbara Barr

Wendy Richardson
Brooklyn Park, Minnesota

Not Quite Black And White

Wendy Richardson has been quilting for 16 years, and has been teaching for about seven. She says of her endeavors: "I thoroughly enjoy these occupations and try to have quilting consume a large part of every day. I also enjoy being a mom to my teenage son, and appreciate his opinions of my work."

first place

1988 AQS Show & Contest
Traditional Pieced, Pro

What Wendy would most like people to know about this award-winning quilt is "how much fun it was!" She explains, "I had no definite plan, other than a thought that the fabrics used would be basically black and white. It just evolved on its own. I like the way the lights and darks change around the quilt; it was a good value exercise for me."

Speaking of the quilt's development, Wendy says, "I thought the quilt was different and fun to look at when I made it. I remember that finding the right border was a problem. But my quilts feel

like children: the more time passes, the more I forget any aggravations or tediousness that may have occurred, and just think – 'Wow! I made that!' "

The quilt is constructed of cottons, and it is hand pieced, except for the border and binding, which were done on the machine. Wendy adds, "The quilting mostly follows the piecing – as in a traditional quilt."

About her award, Wendy says, "This quilt was my first entrance into a national and professional competition. Winning an award definitely boosted my confidence as a quiltmaker and teacher, and was a great experience. I knew I liked what I did, but it is always great to be validated by the public and/or your peers."

To other quiltmakers, Wendy says: "Just do it!"

"The geometric pattern of NOT QUITE BLACK AND WHITE is the Joseph's Coat block, and one day it just said 'make me.'"

NOT QUITE
BLACK AND
WHITE
84" x 84"
©1988
Wendy
Richardson

Martha B. Skelton
Vicksburg, Mississippi

Chips And Whetstones

"Because I used fabrics accumulated from years of sewing for my children and various other home-related projects," says Martha B. Skelton, "I think the overall look of CHIPS AND WHETSTONES is that of an old quilt. I could not have gotten that look from a group of newly purchased pieces."

second place

1988 AQS Show & Contest Traditional Pieced, Pro

Speaking of her quilting history, Martha says: "Born in West Virginia, growing up in Missouri and Oklahoma, and coming to Mississippi in 1947, my quilting reflects that I have quilted most of my life. I began to teach quilting when I left work as a high school librarian in 1971. Reading and an intense interest in the out-of-doors are my other interests, and I use them in my quilting. I am an exhibiting member of the Mississippi Craftsmen's Guild and a small local group of quilters. I enjoy promoting the art of quilting throughout the state."

Martha explains how she developed CHIPS AND WHETSTONES: "Judy Mathieson's book *Mariner's Compass* and my on-going study of antique quilts led me to draft the block pattern and design the applique border to complete the project." Martha used 100% cottons, choosing fabrics at hand. She purchased only the muslin background and the gold print. Further describing the development of the quilt, Martha

adds: "I used a hexagon setting and a combination of hand and machine piecing, appliqueing the red flowers over the points of the hexagons. I used a regular quilting frame."

Looking back at her award, Martha comments, "As a teacher, my making this quilt has encouraged many of my students to learn how to correctly construct Mariner's Compass style patterns and then design their own projects. That alone made my winning bring joy to many women who then brought their projects to completion. It is rewarding to see the varied works resulting from their different personalities."

Martha's advice to other quiltmakers is, "Make your quilt first for the singular pleasure of quiltmaking – to satisfy your individual dream. Enjoy your quiltmaking first and always. Sharing in a competition is an added pleasure. It is helpful for you to see your work in an impersonal setting. Take the judges' comments and go forward from there."

"Setting up a goal to reach in making this quilt helped me. Whenever people start quilts, there should always be goals or reasons toward which they are working."

CHIPS AND
WHETSTONES
80" x 89"
1987
Martha B.
Skelton

Museum of AQS Collection

Shirley Fowlkes
Dallas, Texas

Pulse Star

Shirley Fowlkes says of herself: "I am a fifth generation Texan who grew up on a cattle ranch. I have an art degree and have been quilting for ten years. The majority of my quilts are pictorial applique and the subject matter is usually personal or patriotic."

third place

1988 AQS Show & Contest Traditional Pieced, Pro

"The Lone Star in the center of PULSE STAR," explains Shirley, "is surrounded by 6" and 12" Eight-Pointed Stars. The large Lone Star represents Texas, and the smaller stars represents all the people who settled Texas and made it great." The quilt is pieced of new, 100% cotton fabrics and quilted with outline quilting.

Shirley has received many awards for her quilted clothing, as well as her quilts. In addition, she lectures on quilting, teaches quilting and

also has a line of patterns.

She judges competitions as well. In fact, while judging the Arkansas Show in October 1987, she found herself evaluating a beautiful Lone Star Quilt and commented, "They are so complex, I will never make one." She now adds: "Never say never, because three days later I was in Paducah, Kentucky, buying fabric to make this Lone Star quilt." Shirley says her quilt was inspired by "the beautiful Arkansas contemporary quilt" she had judged and also by "an antique Tennessee quilt."

About her award-winner Shirley says, "I love the quilt now as much as I did then – it is a timeless quilt." She adds, "It has given me great pleasure."

Shirley Fowlkes says: "Set your sights high and go for it!"

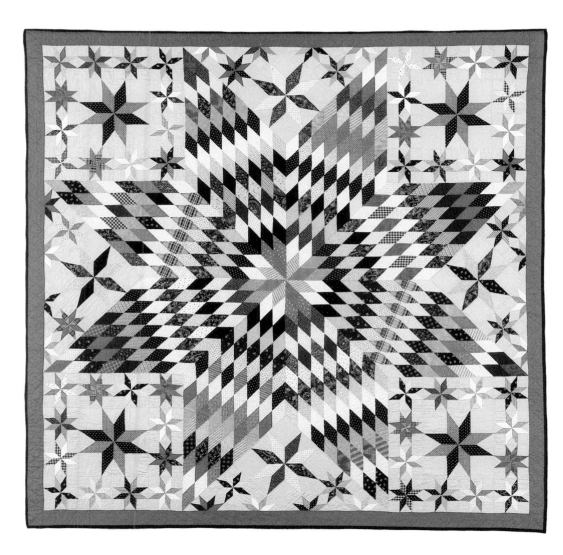

PULSE STAR
87" x 87"
©1988
Shirley Fowlkes

Bobbie Fuhrmann
Lancaster, New York

In Depth

About her award-winning quilt, Bobbie Fuhrmann says, "I was really excited about this quilt when it was just a picture in my mind, and just as excited when I took the last stitch, stepped back, looked at it, and realized that I had accomplished all I set out to do."

first place

1988 AQS Show & Contest Innovative Pieced, Ama

The quilt "takes the traditional Stepping Stones block and applies simple one-point perspective to it, which gives the quilt a dimensional quality." Bobbie says she learned about one-point perspective in her ninth grade art class and "was fascinated by the possibilities even then!"

Constructed of 100% cottons, this quilt was pieced and quilted by hand. Bobbie comments: "It was a very difficult quilt to piece, since the middle part is slightly off-center. This made every piece in the dimensional part a different size. I had to make a full-size drawing of the quilt and cut out separate templates for each piece in that section, making sure that a piece didn't accidentally get turned sideways or upside down as I was cutting and piecing it. Everything was asymetrical and would only fit one way!"

Bobbie holds a B.A. in art and has been quilting since 1977. Speaking of her work, she says, "I specialize in quilts that attempt to use traditional patterns in nontraditional ways. All done by hand, my quilts involve from 3,000 to 7,800 pieces, and take a couple of years to make. I

teach quilt design workshops and lacemaking classes. Although I am also a weaver and a lacemaker, my first love will always be quilting."

About her award, Bobbie says: "Winning first prize at the AQS show was an exhilarating experience. This quilt went on to win a first at the NQA show the following year, was accepted into the 'Visions' show, has been published numerous times, was in two calendars, and has been shown internationally. The biggest effect all this has had on me has been to validate my work. I tend to be a perfectionist and to look at a quilt and find everything wrong with it. This experience has given me more self-confidence and the impetus to work harder to develop my ideas and skills."

To other quilters, Bobbie says: "Keep competitions in perspective. If you're juried into a show or your quilt wins, that doesn't make you the best quiltmaker in the universe. If you aren't accepted or you don't win, it doesn't mean you're not talented. Every quilt is wonderful in its own way."

"IN DEPTH is an example of how you can make innovative quilts with traditional patterns. Rather than looking at a pattern and saying 'I'll make this,' look at it and say, 'What if....' "

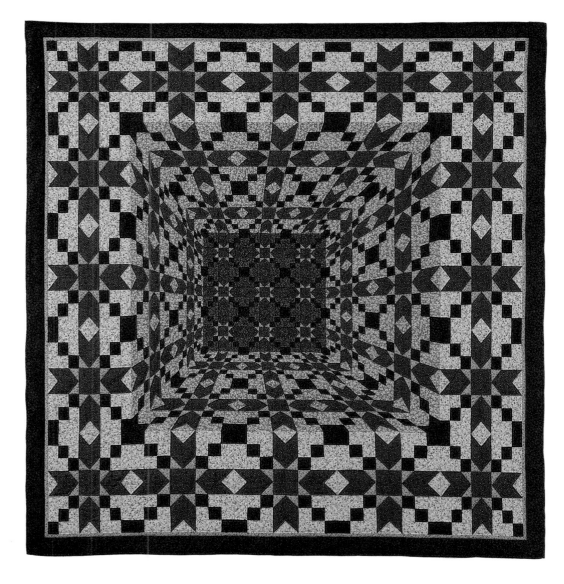

IN DEPTH
73" x 80"
©1988
Bobbie
Fuhrmann

Liesel Niesner
Osnabrück, Germany

Einsamkeit

Speaking of the development of EINSAMKEIT, Liesel Niesner says, "The design came to mind during our holidays in Switzerland, where I again became alarmed about our fragile environment. I had the idea of a totally empty landscape without any living creature, divided from the living by a huge fence."

second place

1988 AQS Show & Contest Innovative Pieced, Ama

This quilt, constructed of 100% cotton fabrics, is the realization of that idea. Liesel comments: "From the beginning of my love for quilting, I have liked to sew in blocks. For about six years I had been searching for a way of continuing that, but at the same time making quilts in which the blocks were hidden. On one of our holidays, I realized it would be possible to combine those two goals."

She explains, "EINSAMKEIT is sewn in 25 rectangular, equally divided blocks. I was satisfied. Since then, I've sewn about ten quilts using this special technique, and there are more in my mind."

Liesel describes herself as being "absolutely self-taught." She adds, "I've hand quilted all of my quilts; I enjoy that for relaxation. But, because I've never had lessons, I didn't know anything about quilting hoops or frames. So I figured out a method to quilt on my lap with only the help of three pins."

Liesel's work has been exhibited often, and since 1979 she has been involved in many one-woman and group shows. She has completed about 115 quilts, most large in size. She also lectures and teaches quilt classes and workshops.

Speaking of her award, Liesel says, "This was my first quilt to win an award. Before that time I would never have dreamed of such a possibility." She continues, "The award has not had much influence on my life, except to give great pleasure." She adds, "But from that time on, I felt highly encouraged to enter more competitions, and my self-confidence has grown a little, because I think: 'The jury of AQS must know about quilts.'"

"I hope that EINSAMKEIT will remind people to be careful with their environment, to preserve it for future generations."

EINSAMKEIT
85" x 60"
©1987
Liesel Niesner

To others making quilts, Liesel says: "When someone has fallen in love with quilting, she has to start. If she prefers to take classes, she should do it in that way. The more she quilts and takes classes, the more she learns. She can't sit down and say, 'Now I'm doing a masterpiece.' She needs to continue working, and suddenly one day she will send in slides for a competition. I like the saying, 'If anything is worth doing, it is worth doing well.' "

Joyce Buchberger
Chandler, Arizona

Duet

Joyce Buchberger explains that she had taken a class in curved two-patch from Joyce Schlotzhauer just before making this quilt. She adds, "I'd taken this class, but I hate flowers: I'm just not a floral person. I thought something else could be done with that type of design. This quilt was my experiment with that idea."

third place

1988 AQS Show & Contest Innovative Pieced, Ama

Joyce continues, "The quilt is hand and machine pieced with a range of fabrics, including cottons, velvets, satins, and brocades. Both right and wrong sides were used. I used whatever gave me the right shades." The quilt was hand quilted.

This, Joyce reveals, was actually only the second full-size quilt she had done. She explains, "I love all needle arts, except knitting. Quilt-

ing has not been a tradition in my family, but I am a little bit on the frugal side. I had sewed for years and could not bear throwing out the little bits left after sewing." Joyce adds, "I have continued making quilts, and have gone on to win other awards. My quilts are all originals and they have appeared in a number of publications. I am active in guilds, and we have started our own clothing company." Joyce explains, "I

always use 'we' because my husband is so involved in the quilting and clothing."

Joyce wishes people could see DUET in person: "If it's not viewed up close, you miss a lot of the unique quilting lines in it. Photos don't show the lines very well. The quilting doesn't follow the patchwork pattern."

About her award, Joyce says, "This award gave me the courage to go on to subsequent pieces. One of the pieces we had in the show a few years ago was pleated, fringed, beaded, and had patchwork in it. This award gave me permission to set no limitations, no restrictions."

Speaking to others, Joyce says, "I'm a strong advocate of entering a judged show. How else can you get such valuable advice on how to improve your quilts? A local judged show is a wonderful way to receive constructive advice. Don't limit yourself to what you have already seen done. Do something that hasn't been done."

"Though this quilt won third prize at the AQS Show, it won first everywhere else it went. Even if your quilt doesn't place in a particular show, send it to the next show. Don't let the ranking by one set of judges be a determining factor."

DUET
73" x 80"
©1988
Joyce
Buchberger

Caryl Bryer Fallert
Oswego, Illinois

Chromatic Progressions: Autumn

Speaking of CHROMATIC PROGRESSIONS: AUTUMN, Caryl Bryer Fallert comments: "This is a quilt that has been away from home almost from the day it was completed. After the AQS show, it traveled for a year and a half in the 1988 'Needle Expressions' show, then went from one show to another for almost a year. It is currently in a three-year traveling exhibit called 'The Definitive Contemporary American Quilt,' organized by the Bernice Steinbaum Gallery in New York City."

first place

1988 AQS Show & Contest
Innovative Pieced, Pro

Describing the quilt, Caryl continues, "This quilt is the eleventh in a series of quilts which incorporate constructed three-dimensional tucks into pieced backgrounds. The tucks are constructed of cotton fabric dyed in color progressions, and they are a different color on each side. A second color progression is used in the

background of the interlacing arcs and in the outside border. The use of color progressions and the twisting of the tucks create the illusion of movement in the foreground.

"The colorful arcs are juxtaposed against a rather static background pieced in shades of brown. The use of browns and rather muted color gradations suggests the feeling of a crisp, sunny, autumn day. The traditional Dove in the Window quilt block used on the back of this contemporary quilt is my tribute to the anonymous quilt artists of the past."

Caryl adds, "The quilt

top, with its curving bands of tucks, proved to be technically very difficult to assemble, so it was Spring 1991 before I made the second quilt in this series, CHROMATIC PROGRESSIONS #2.

During the past five years, Caryl has become known for her unusual and striking works of fabric art. Her award-winning quilts have been in numerous national and international juried exhibits across the U.S., as well as in Japan, Australia, Europe, and Russia. Her work is also included in a number of private, corporate, and public collections. In 1969, Caryl received her B.A. from Wheaton College. She also studied art at Illinois State University, University of Wisconsin, and College of DuPage. Her studio is in her 113-year-old farm house in northern Illinois.

Speaking of her feelings about her work, Caryl says: "When I am making a quilt I am usually totally focused on the creative process, and that is the most important thing to me. After the quilt is finished, the most important thing to me is for other peo-

"CHROMATIC PROGRESSIONS: AUTUMN was my first attempt to combine string piecing and three-dimensional tucks, two techniques I have used extensively in my quilts."

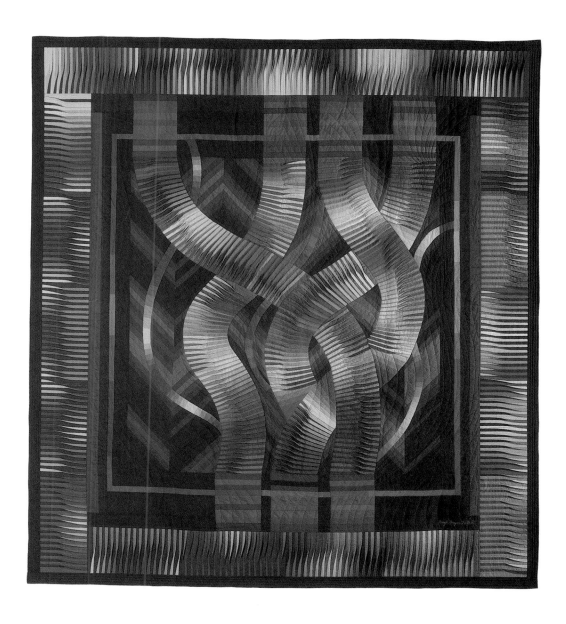

CHROMATIC
PROGRESSIONS:
AUTUMN
87" x 96"
©1988
Caryl Bryer
Fallert

ple to enjoy it. I can let it go. I am happy when my quilts are on exhibit, or when they find new homes with people who love them."

Her advice to quilters: "If you have more ideas than time, use the design ideas that please you the most and that are the most personal first. These will almost always please others as well."

Linda MacDonald
Willits, California

Clear Palisades

Commenting on her work, Linda MacDonald explains, "CLEAR PALISADES is an original landscape design, reminiscent of palisades running near an ocean." She adds, "I'm concerned with creating conflict in the three-dimensional shapes by having them recede and yet look as if they are falling forward."

second place

1988 AQS Show & Contest Innovative Pieced, Pro

The quilt is constructed of cotton solids. Linda adds that "everything was pieced by machine" and "most of the fabric was dyed with Procion™ MX dyes."

The quilting was all done by hand. Asked what she would like people to know about CLEAR PALISADES, Linda replies: "Some of the quilting includes small geometric shapes and insect-like creatures." She adds: "This quilt was just about the last one of my large illusionistic pieces. They take a long time to make, are large, and are difficult to piece. I've recently been more concerned with

smaller pieces that explore different avenues: surface textures, overlayers of grids, responding to chance through paint and stitch."

Linda holds a B.A. in art from San Francisco State University, and is presently pursuing an M.F.A. in textiles at the same university. She also holds a single subject credential in art and has taught art in high school since 1985. She teaches at symposiums and art centers during the summer.

To other quiltmakers, Linda says: "Don't make quilts for particular shows – just make the pieces that you really want to make. There are enough shows out there for you to choose one that's right for you. Periodically, forget about the quilts you have made before and make something completely new."

To other quiltmakers, Linda MacDonald says: "Always do your best work. You are your most important audience."

CLEAR
PALISADES
92" x 92"
©1988
Linda
MacDonald

Alison Goss
Hockessin, Delaware

Looking For The Inner Light

Alison Goss fell in love with quilts in the late 1970's, and has been teaching since 1980. She has a varied background as an elementary school teacher, production sewer, environmentalist, wife, and mother, all of which have helped her create quilts and share her ideas with others. Her quilts have won many awards, including

third place

1988 AQS Show & Contest Innovative Pieced, Pro

Best Wall Quilt at the 1991 AQS show; her wearables have been included in the Fairfield-Concord Fashion Show four years. She loves playing with color and finding new ways to create depth and dimension in her quilts.

About the development of LOOKING FOR THE INNER LIGHT, Alison says, "This design emerged from a series of drawing exercises I worked through, using Betty Edward's book, *Drawing on the Artist Within*, as a guide. The design is based on triangles which are subdivided into thirds. Careful use of light, medium and dark values within each triangle gives the dimensional effect."

Constructed of 100% cottons, the quilt is machine pieced and hand quilted. Alison adds: "I decided on the overall dimensions for the light, medium and dark sections of triangles, then drew the triangles for each section on paper. I used these triangles as pattern pieces, cutting them up and using them as templates as I worked through the piecing. This allowed me to make the cut triangles any size I wanted (no two are the same), knowing that they would fit together when sewn."

Talking about the development of the quilt, Alison says, "When I first started the piecing I became very excited about the depth I saw, and about the secondary shapes that emerged when I sewed several triangles together. Then I read an article in a quilt magazine that set out rules for deciding whether or not a design was good. Of course, my design broke a number of 'rules,' especially the one about not letting too many points come together in one place, but by then I was

"You should make a quilt to express something important to you and you should make it to satisfy yourself, without worrying about how others will judge it. Then you will love it, whether or not it wins an award in a competition."

LOOKING FOR
THE INNER
LIGHT
96" x 84"
©1987
Alison Goss

determined to make the quilt, so I ignored the article.

Looking at the quilt now, Alison explains, "My feeling about the quilt hasn't really changed, although I have found it 'moodier' than I expected it to be. It can be very dark and somber, or quite bright and cheerful, depending on the lighting conditions.

"This quilt marked a real change from the bargello quilts I had been making," Alison explains. "It was the first of a series I am still working on, exploring possibilities for depth and dimension with triangles. I was thrilled to win the award, and it helped me continue to work in this new direction with more confidence."

Audree L. Sells
Chaska, Minnesota

Javanese Jungle

"This quilt," says maker Audree L. Sells, "was my first attempt at pictorial applique." She continues, "I began quilting in 1986 with very little knowledge of what was going on in the contemporary quilt world. I had taught elementary school for 33 years and my hobby was painting. In Spring 1986 I attended a Minnesota Quilters Show and Conference – and that was the beginning of my 'quilt career.' I was so inspired by the beautiful and amazing things quilters were doing that there has been no stopping me ever since."

first place

*1988 AQS Show & Contest
Applique, Amateur*

Speaking of JAVANESE JUNGLE, Audree says, "The design was adapted from an original batik by Emilie VonKerchoff, a Dutch artist known for her paintings and batiks. It was featured on the cover of *Needlecraft: The Home Arts Magazine*, November 1933. I liked the flowing design, unusual flora and 'old' looking colors."

Audree adds, "I tried to find fabric that had a faded look and selected hand-dyed fabrics, all-cotton for the most part, and a few prints, for interest. I worked the quilt in four sections. The details on the animals were done in embroidery stitches."

Looking back at the quilt, Audree comments: "This

quilt was my first in a series of pictorial quilts. I really didn't know what I was doing when I made this quilt – there are so many things I know how to do better now, after having made this one and five others since. Experience is a great teacher and my method of learning has been the discovery method!"

Speaking of her award, Audree says, "It took me a year to make this quilt and a lot of courage to enter it in the AQS competition. Winning that award gave me the confidence to go on and try some other quilting techniques, get others started in quilting and make dozens of new friends – all 'serious' quilters."

To other quiltmakers Audree says, "So many quilters I've met have unfinished projects. My advice is – when you have that inspiration, GO TO IT. Begin the project and stay with it until it is finished. That's the only thing accepted in competition: a finished product."

"Competition isn't for everyone, but it has taught me to do my very best, and it has also shown me that sometimes even that isn't good enough."

JAVANESE
JUNGLE
75" x 94"
1987
Audree L. Sells

Museum of AQS Collection

Karen Keller
Chrisman, Illinois

Once Upon A Time...

Karen Keller says of her quilting background, "My first quilt was a patchwork blue-jean quilt. I ended up tying it because I found it impossible to quilt. My next quilt was blue-jean applique. I eliminated seams and quilted it. After I started ONCE UPON A TIME... in 1978, and before I finished it in 1986, I made another applique quilt and a wall-hanging from blue jeans."

second place

1988 AQS Show & Contest Applique, Amateur

"The castle in ONCE UPON A TIME...," explains Karen, "is a combination of many of the castles in my childhood story books. I first drew an overall design on graph paper and then enlarged each piece for my patterns." She adds, "The quilt top is 100% denim from old blue jeans – construction was a massive undertaking! I had to use the stab stitch for quilting – one stitch at a time, often using needle holders to make that stitch."

Speaking of the development of this quilt, Karen says, "After the AQS show I was questioned about from where the idea for ONCE UPON A TIME... came. I usually told people it grew out of my childhood storybooks,

but after being asked many times, I finally had to ask myself from just where this quilt had come. My answer now is that this quilt comes from my innermost self, a safe, warm place spun from the fairy tales of childhood. I didn't realize this until years after the quilt was made."

Asked about the effect of her award, Karen comments, "Since the AQS show, I've joined our local quilters' group and met a lot of wonderful people, and I've learned a great deal about quiltmaking."

Asked to give advice to other quiltmakers, Karen says: "Make what makes you happy. When you feel stuck, leave it to your higher power and come back to it later. Don't worry; it will work out! As for as entering competitions, nothing has ever shown me how much I have to learn as clearly as entering competitions has."

*"I made ONCE UPON A TIME... because I wanted to win
the pretty purple Best of Show ribbon at the local Georgetown Fair.
I made it, and I did win the pretty purple ribbon!"*

ONCE UPON
A TIME...
63" x 81"
1986
Karen Keller

Eleanor J. Carlson
Cadillac, Michigan

Cinderella

Of the development of this quilt, Eleanor J. Carlson says: "I had no pattern for it, but got ideas from many sources: magazines, coloring books, other books. I feel the Lord gave me the idea and the influences, as they came from many people and places."

She continues, "I had never made a picture quilt before, nor had I ever studied art. So I had to practice making the shapes several times before the pieces were correct in size and color."

third place

1988 AQS Show & Contest
Applique, Amateur

Eleanor comments further on the quilt's development: "When I was still working on it, the Lord impressed upon me I hadn't made this quilt myself. He had given it to me and it was a composite of the Rapture of the Church and Second Coming. This Lord is in heaven, the doors are about to open, the midnight hour has struck. He will come in all His Glory, the angels with Him. God's love never ends, like my border, a continuous cable. He has no beginning or end."

Eleanor would like people viewing her quilt to realize

that "God works in unusual ways, or can take the ordinary and do extra-ordinary things with it for His Glory." Speaking of the AQS award her quilt won, Eleanor adds, "I feel it's God given – His tangible gift to me to show and show to all. He chose me to do this, too. Even though it won Best of Show at Dollywood and the prize was a substantial purchase award, I waived my right to accept the award and chose to keep the quilt so I can freely talk to people at churches or groups and tell and show them this story. It inspires all who see it."

Eleanor says to other quiltmakers, "Use the talent God has given each of you and improve it. If you find you pay chose attention to detail and workmanship, then compare your work to others in competition, and you may be surprised by how well you have done."

"Although I did all the work on CINDERELLA, people's ideas were jewels to grasp, and I was wise enough in my ignorance that I knew I needed the help, from whatever place it came."

CINDERELLA
74" x 88"
1988
Eleanor J.
Carlson

Faye Anderson
Denver, Colorado

My Mother Taught Me To Sew

Speaking of the development of MY MOTHER TAUGHT ME TO SEW, Faye Anderson explains, "The composition is inspired by an 1870 quilt made by Hannah Riddle of Woolwich, Maine. Nearly all of the block designs are repeated twice, once in bright colors and once in grayed tones."

first place

1988 AQS Show & Contest
Applique, Pro

The blocks are hand appliqued, hand embroidered and hand quilted. The fabrics used are 100% cotton fabrics, and flat sequins have been added to embellish a number of the blocks.

Faye Anderson was born

in Elmhurst, IL. She holds a B.F.A. in graphic design from the University of Denver, and began quilting in 1980 as a result of a sampler class at a local quilt shop. She makes traditional and innovative quilts and clothing.

Asked what she would like others to know, she says: "Applique does not need to be tedious. This work was done using the needle-turn method presented in my book *Applique Designs: My Mother Taught Me to Sew*. This method involves no basting or freezer paper, spray starch, etc. I find doing handwork more relaxing than working at the sewing machine."

To other quiltmakers, Faye says: "Quilts take a L-O-N-G time to make. Don't be impatient to get started. Take time and care in planning. It is time well spent. Color value is as important as hue when you are developing the color palette for a quilt."

She adds, "I love competitions because they encourage innovation, creativity, and excellence in craftsmanship."

"I'm pleased that I was able to find a tangible way to show my mother how much her guidance and encouragement have meant to me creatively. This seems to be a sentiment shared by many other quiltmakers."

MY MOTHER
TAUGHT ME
TO SEW
82" x 95"
©1988
Faye Anderson

Mary Chartier
New London, Connecticut

Morning Glory

Mary Chartier says of the development of MORNING GLORY: "This quilt was based on "Techny Chimes," a Nancy Pearson design which I fell in love with the first time I saw it. I knew right away that someday I would have to make a quilt using that beautiful design."

second place

1988 AQS Show & Contest
Applique, Pro

She continues, "This quilt was made mostly of scraps I'd bought for other quilts. I stenciled the flowers to give them a three-dimensional look, and used a poly-cotton blend for the background (which I probably wouldn't do again). Sometimes working within constraints of one kind or another forces you to become more creative. For example, I didn't extend the vine in the four corners all the way around the border because I ran out of the green fabric for the leaves and stems!"

Speaking of her background, Mary says, "I am a National Quilting Association certified quiltmaking teacher. I have been quilting for about twenty years and am now back in Connecticut after spending a wonderful five years quilting with the nicest people. Though I'm presently working full-time, I look forward to quilting and teaching very soon."

About her award, Mary says, "It made me very humble. I still cannot figure out how I ever won second place in one of the greatest contests in the country. In the future, however, I want to settle down to making simple quilts which look like they belong on a bed, and leave competition to the really talented quilters out there."

Mary recommends to other quiltmakers: "Make your quilt to please yourself, and don't worry about whether judges will like the design, the colors, the fabric." Mary adds, "However, I find I do a better job technically (in the piecing, the appliqueing, etc.) when I know a judge is going to be examining my quilt."

"This quilt was a pure joy to work on. Making a quilt with a Nancy Pearson design is like playing the most beautiful music you've ever heard."

MORNING
GLORY
80" x 100"
1987
Mary Chartier

Museum of AQS Collection

Dawn E. Amos
Rapid City, South Dakota

Before The Crossing

Speaking of the development of this award-winning quilt, Dawn E. Amos says, "I drew my own patterns, sketching from photographs, paintings, etc." She then constructed the quilt using 100% cotton muslin for the background and hand-dyed fabrics for the realistic applique. The entire quilt was then hand quilted.

third place

1988 AQS Show & Contest
Applique, Pro

BEFORE THE CROSSING tells of the Native American's simple life before he crossed paths with the white man. Dawn explains, "BEFORE THE CROSSING was the second in a series of two quilts. The first one was CROSSING PATH, which depicted a Native American and white settler along with horses, buffalo, tepees, log cabins, eagles and a wagon train. CROSSING PATH was disqualified from competition because it was an inch too narrow. Thus, BEFORE THE CROSSING was created (it was an attempt to redeem myself!). I still have trouble controlling the finished size of the quilt and prefer not to have any size limitations imposed."

Asked if she feels any differently about this quilt now than she did when she first made it, Dawn replies, "Sure, it is like an old painting you have in the closet, which you don't want anyone to see. I feel as if I've improved with each quilt I've done and have so much yet to learn." Dawn adds, "My hope is that by the time I'm 60 years old, I'll be pretty good at it."

To other quiltmakers, Dawn Amos says: "Enter shows,
and go to see them if it is at all possible for you.
There is a lot of learning that can be done by just observing."

BEFORE THE
CROSSING
64" x 88"
1988
Dawn E. Amos

Jan Lanahan
Walkersville, Maryland

Earth Mother

"EARTH MOTHER," says maker Jan Lanahan, "was of my own design. Seminole patchwork is used to depict layers of earth, water, rock, etc. The focal point of the quilt is the Earth Mother, who is sowing corn."

Cottons which have been dyed and over-dyed are used in this quilt, which is constructed of Seminole patchwork, with the central figure accomplished through reverse applique. The pots are made using both applique and reverse applique.

first place

*1988 AQS Show & Contest
Other Techniques, Ama*

There are many things Jan says she would like viewers to know about this quilt: "It has many secrets. Rows of Seminole patchwork represent layers of earth, rock, underground water, soil, corn, trees and mountains. The quilting is entirely by hand. I quilted rows of animals starting with reptiles, and moving on to bugs, mountain goats, horses, bears, and the highest deity, the eagle, in the clouds."

Jan says of her background, "I was born and raised in Australia. I met my husband, Mike, there; he was serving in the United States Air Force. We moved to the

States, where he was stationed in Phoenix, AZ. I was fascinated with Native American history, folklore, arts – everything about them. This fascination has stayed with me over the years. I've taught myself how to spin wool into yarn and have also learned natural dyeing, weaving, and coiled basketry. All of this has influenced me in my quilting."

Asked if the award and competition has had an effect on her life, Jan comments: "After winning at AQS with this quilt and another quilt, BASKETS AND THE CORN, I tried making commissioned quilts as a living for a year. I loved it, but financially it was a loss, so I went to work in an antiques mall selling antique quilts along with many other antique items. I now manage that mall."

About quiltmaking in general, Jan says, "You have to be dedicated."

"When I was making this quilt, it took over my every waking hour. Now, when I can look at it with detachment, I think I enjoy it more."

EARTH
MOTHER
82" x 96"
1987
Jan Lanahan

E. Celine Doster
Montgomery, Texas

Working Hands Happy Hearts

E. Celine Doster explains the origins of this quilt as follows: "It was made after seeing another scrap Log Cabin quilt. After getting the blocks made, though, I thought it was boring, so I added the stenciled blocks and set the blocks on-point." The quilt is made with 100% cotton fabric, and it is machine pieced, hand stenciled with acrylic paints, and hand quilted.

second place

*1988 AQS Show & Contest
Other Techniques, Ama*

Speaking of her background, Celine says, "I have been quilting since 1981, and am basically self taught. Inspired and supported by friends, I began to stencil on fabric. I now teach classes in stenciling and quilting at local shops."

"I have been married 20 years, and have a daughter and a son. My husband, Steve, is a full-time musician (lead guitar) and has given me lots of freedom to be me. I also work part-time." Celine adds, "I want to design and make quilts to leave to my children. I have also designed a couple of patterns. I hope to eventually work full-time in the quilting world that I love."

Commenting on her feelings about WORKING HANDS HAPPY HEARTS, Celine says, "I have come to value it more because of the memories associated with it." She adds that the quilt and its award have had an effect on her life. She explains, "People who have never met me sometimes know me through my quilt."

She continues, "I also feel that perhaps 100 years down the road someone will be able to say, 'My great, great, grandmother made these quilts and just look at all the awards she won,' and will be proud to know this."

To others, Celine says: "Make quilts for yourself, do the best work you can do on each one, and above all, love them. That love will show. If you are competitive, enter shows. Competition sometimes makes you strive harder to do your best work."

*Asked what she would most like people to know about her quilt,
E. Celine Doster replied: "That WORKING HANDS HAPPY HEARTS
was the first quilt I completed all by myself, and that if I can do it,
they can do it."*

WORKING
HANDS
HAPPY
HEARTS
88" x 88"
1987
E. Celine
Doster

Diane Guzman
Fillmore, California

David's Quilt

Diane Guzman says the original design for this quilt was inspired by her husband's love of music. She explains: "The musical scale, instruments and notes are original designs which I hand painted with fabric paint." The quilt is machine pieced and hand quilted.

third place

1988 AQS Show & Contest Other Techniques, Ama

Originally from Flint, Michigan, Diane studied interior design and art history. She adds, "I have always enjoyed painting, drawing, and sewing."

Looking at DAVID'S QUILT today, Diane comments, "My style has matured somewhat and now I am sure there are many things I would have done differently, but I still like it very much." She continues, speaking of the effect of the quilt's award, "I have

gone on to make many more quilts, and have begun exhibiting my work at art galleries. I believe entering the show gave me the confidence to do that. In November 1991 I was a featured artist in two very prominent Los Angeles galleries."

Talking to other quiltmakers, Diane says: "A mistake I have made more than once is that I tend to get bored after working on a quilt for a long time and want to hurry up and finish it so I can start something else. I have always regretted the times I have done that. I have found it is better to put the quilt aside and finish it when I'm ready; it's okay to have twenty projects going at once."

"The fabric designs on DAVID'S QUILT are hand painted. When people see my quilts, they often want to know how I find material with these unusual designs on it."

DAVID'S QUILT
90" x 78"
1987
Diane (Pounds)
Guzman

Vicki Johnson
Soquel, California

A Bright Winter Day In Mendocino

This design is an original, which maker Vicki Johnson says was "influenced by living for eight years on the Mendocino Coast." She adds, "Mendocino is a small coastal town in northern California. Almost a ghost town in the fifties, it has been preserved as a turn-of-the-century logging town. Now, as a resort area, it has many artists and craftspeople living and working there. In this quilt I wanted to show the open airy feeling of walking on the headlands and looking back at the town."

first place

1988 AQS Show & Contest Other Techniques, Pro

Vicki explains the development of the quilt: "First the ocean, cliffs and trees were painted with Versatex™ fabric paints. Then I appliqued the buildings and logs on with soft-edge machine applique. The sky and border were added using more traditional techniques. I really just built them around the painting, using squares. The logs were repeated with strip piecing. The top was machine quilted with extra-loft batting."

A BRIGHT WINTER DAY IN MENDOCINO is one of a series of painted quilts Vicki has done on Mendocino. She adds, "Now I am doing underwater, barn and lighthouse quilts, using these same techniques of painting and soft-edge applique."

Looking at BRIGHT WINTER DAY IN MENDOCINO now, Vicki remarks, "It reminds me of the feeling of seeking a community that I had when I lived in Mendocino. Now, though, I could do a much better quilt, because

my skill has improved a lot since then." Vicki has been creating quilted and painted artworks since 1970. She holds a degree in graphic design from the University of Michigan, and worked in that field for ten years before devoting her time to quilts. Her works have been included in many exhibits and collections.

Vicki finds that this quilt and its award have helped her build a teaching career. She explains, "I've recently flown off to my first big out-of-state quilt conference. This quilt was directly responsible for this teaching opportunity and for the article which appeared in *American Quilter* magazine. Before, I was teaching around California, but now people in other states know about my work."

To other quiltmakers, Vicki recommends: "Do it! Follow your own ideas wherever they lead you. That is the most exciting thing happening with quilts today. Once you have a quilt that you feel is unique, don't hesitate to send it off to exhibits. You will be amazed at what can happen."

"I have learned something from each quilt I make."

A BRIGHT
WINTER DAY
IN MENDOCINO
65" x 82"
©1985
Vicki L.
Johnson

Anne J. Oliver
Alexandria, Virginia

Look Up, It's A Metal Ceiling

Anne J. Oliver explains that the patterns for this award winner were "created with freezer paper and based on a salesman's book of tin ceiling plates from the turn of the century. Most patterns were simplified to make them suitable for quilting, and various types of quilting were used."

second place

*1988 AQS Show & Contest
Other Techniques, Pro*

For the whole-cloth, seamless quilt top, 100% cotton fabric was used, with an extra loft batt. Describing the creation of the quilt, Anne says, "To create highs and lows, various types of quilting were used (crosshatch, meandering, echoing). The work was done in a 22" hoop with no stand. A corner of the living room couch was mine. It took about 1,000 hours to create, quilt, and finish off LOOK UP, IT'S A METAL CEILING."

Anne started quilting in the mid-1970's. She says of herself, "I would call myself a frustrated oil painter. My work looked correct, but it just didn't have the 'oomph' that quilting brings about." She adds that she has "no formal background, just smatterings of art courses." Most of what she knows she says she "learned by trial and error – lots of it."

Anne does not feel quilts should be pigeon-holed as crafts, bedspreads, etc. She explains, "They can be traditional or contemporary works of art, for the wall, not the bed. This quilt crosses over into the art field for me, yet, by the time it passes into the hands of the next generation, it will be traditional. It is a quilt of our times, not contemporary, but traditional. It has opened up a new facet of quilting for me. It has forced me to think about different ways to present my work, in other words, to take quilts out of the bedroom."

Speaking of her thoughts about the quilt today, Anne says, "It is not in my possession, being the first art piece I sold. The fact that someone specially purchased this piece meant it served its purpose well. I found I was able to say goodbye to this favorite piece when it was time for it to leave my possession. It took me to Europe for 26 days, where I stayed with quilters. I will never forget the trip or the quilt; I have fond memories to replace its loss."

About competitions, Anne says, "AQS and other competitions of its kind are my 'peers.' They are my catalysts – from design to finish – for a piece of work. No other incentive serves the purpose as well. I have received much mail from past viewers. It proves that people do appreciate these shows and glean much information from them, even if only from viewing the quilts."

Anne advises other quilt-makers: "Enter shows for self-esteem, confidence, and experience. What better way is there to break the procrastination habit. Also, narrow your goals. Twenty unfinished pieces in the closet more than equal one finished quilt, but who wants to look at unfinished pieces!"

"The length of time it takes me to complete my quilts ranges from a year to eighteen months, about 1,100 hours. The infinite patience I've had to develop carries over into other things I do, except for dusting and basting."

LOOK UP,
IT'S A METAL
CEILING
80" x 80"
1987
Anne J. Oliver

Private Collection,
Washington, D.C.

Flavil Patton
Venice, Florida

Spring Flowers

Flavil Patton explains that the center of this stunning trapuntoed quilt was a purchased pattern. He says that he did the quilt as if he were "doing a painting."

The center features a group of daffodils, encircled by rings of daffodils and other flowers. Six-inch circles were then added to complete the quilt at its edges.

third place

1988 AQS Show & Contest
Other Techniques, Pro

Flavil comments: "As I worked on the center circles, I saw that I would soon have too busy a pattern. So I added the plain circle. All this was done on a mathematic scale. Each circle was figured to fit the pattern to be made. The corners include a small pattern I found in a magazine. I had had my binding on other projects described as irregular, so I made this border scalloped."

Flavil, a retired banker, decided fourteen years ago to continue his grandmother's and mother's quilting tradition. He was living in Florida at the time, and had become bored. He had "picked up seashells until they were spilling out of the cupboards." He went downtown, selected prints he liked, then found solids to coordinate, and his first quilt was soon underway. Flavil had sewed as a child. He explains, "When I grew up you had to make your own entertainment, so you did whatever your mother did."

Flavil learned a little sewing in that way, but had not sewed since childhood.

When he returned to Tennessee, he visited Mildred Locke to see some quilts she had, and soon he was involved in her classes. Flavil comments, "She was one of the people who helped me go forward in quilting." He took classes and then began creating quilts, one of which is SPRING FLOWERS. His greatest hope is that those viewing this quilt will "treat it as a painting."

Flavil explains that this quilt was not fully designed and then made, but rather it was designed as he sewed it. He comments, "I bought the center piece. At once point I had heard of stippling, so I decided I'd stipple the center of it. Later, I decided to use a rose pattern I had. I designed the quilt as I went."

Speaking of quilting, Flavil says, "It is a good pastime for someone who has time." He adds, "I have three rooms: a music room, a quilting room and a whittling room. I have lots to keep me busy."

Flavil Patton's advice to other quiltmakers is simple: "Keep on keeping on."

SPRING
FLOWERS
86" x 88"
1987
Flavil Patton

Jan Lanahan
Walkersville, Maryland

Baskets And The Corn

Jan Lanahan explains that this quilt is an original design. She comments, "This evolved after finishing another quilt, EARTH MOTHER (pages 48-49), in which I had used Seminole patchwork in rows to represent layers of earth. It hit me that I could 'build' Native American basket designs using this technique."

first place

1988 AQS Show & Contest Theme: Baskets

Jan continues, "I used natural fiber fabrics, such as cottons and linens, to make row after row of tiny Seminole patchwork and added a group of coiled baskets in the center, hand painted with dyes."

Asked what she would most like people to know when viewing this quilt, Jan says, "Baskets, especially corn baskets, were so important to early man that the Native Americans raised this utilitarian object to an art

form. The basket was used to store corn, their lifeline during winter months. The brown background is the red soil of the Southwest."

Speaking of her background, Jan says, "My husband and I and our daughters have toured the world, courtesy of the United States Air Force. We have lived in some strange and wonderful places. I have found each and every experience invaluable in my quiltmaking."

Jan adds, "My love of quilts old and new led me to apply for a job as a sales person in an antiques mall where many quilts are bought and sold. I now manage that mall."

Her suggestion for other quiltmakers is: "Patience."

"The basket theme was a natural for me. My interest in Native American culture had earlier led to my learning to make coiled baskets."

BASKETS AND
THE CORN
67" x 80"
1988
Jan Lanahan

Museum of AQS Collection

Sara Ann McLennand
Wellington, Florida

Duck Island Basket

The original design for this quilt, says maker Sara Ann McLennand, was "influenced by a Native American basket in my grandmother's cabin on Duck Island in Copper Harbor (upper peninsula), Michigan. She adds that this was, in fact, the first in a series of quilts based on Native American designs.

second place

1988 AQS Show & Contest Theme: Baskets

Chintz fabrics were used in the quilt's construction, and Sara Ann explains that she uses freezer paper piecing. She sews by hand for accuracy when the design involves small pieces.

About her background, she says, "I am a self taught quilter of 18 years. I have an art background, and love geometric designs. This was the first quilt I ever did that was not a traditional pattern! I have been doing original work ever since. I continue to enjoy experimenting with color and fabric, design and texture. Quilting is a great

medium. It has allowed me to combine my artistic creativity and sewing skills."

Sara Ann says she appreciates DUCK ISLAND BASKET for "what it is." She adds, "I realize that I can look at it more objectively now with regards to some of the technical aspects; however, I love this quilt. My grandparents' cabin was (and still is) a very special place, and since the basket came from there, it naturally reminds me of the summers I spent there."

Speaking of the competition, Sara Ann says, "The AQS show with its basket theme was the best thing to ever

happen to me. Throughout my quilting life, I had done traditional patterns (through which I learned), and my quilting was interrupted by other priorities such as having children, or moving from Illinois to Florida. My growth was just so slow! Then I heard of the AQS show: I now had a deadline to meet, a chance to create something of my own – and the knowledge it had to be good! What a wonderful challenge.

"When my quilt won second place, I couldn't believe it! I was almost overwhelmed. This show was such an inspiration. It was the spark that I needed to be really serious about my work. It was the beginning. I have since won various other awards, both locally and nationally, and I continue to grow."

To other quiltmakers, Sara Ann says, "Take your craft seriously, but not to the point where it becomes tedious. Have some fun! Competitions are excellent, but their value and effect depend on where you are with your work, and why you are entering. Are you entering for the money? Are you

"Native American basket designs can be a great source of inspiration for quilts. It's fun to take a woven design and transfer aspects of it to flat color."

DUCK ISLAND
BASKET
80" x 80"
1988
Sara Ann
McLennand

entering with hopes of some constructive criticism? Are you entering just for the heck of it? All are okay, but not all competitions are the same. You probably already know where your strengths and weaknesses are. Chances are judges aren't going to tell you something you don't already know, even if they have the time! Ultimately, I would say: go for it! You have just as good a chance of winning as anybody else."

Elsie Vredenburg
Tustin, Michigan

Amish Easter Baskets

Elsie Vredenburg based her quilt top's design on an antique quilt that featured the traditional Cake Stand pattern. As she developed her own quilt, she changed the size and then designed her own quilting.

The quilt is made of 100% cotton, and Elsie says she used rotary cutting where possible and quick-piece machine methods. The Sawtooth edging is hand appliqued and the entire quilt is hand quilted.

third place

1988 AQS Show & Contest Theme: Baskets

Married, with three grown children and four grandchildren, Elsie is a former home economics teacher who has been quilting for over 30 years, 15 years seriously. She comments, "The 1976 bicentennial was probably the thing that really got me going as a quilter. For ten or twelve years, I sold quilts and other quilted items at arts and crafts shows. The 1988 AQS show was really the first contest I had ever entered, except for a couple of local shows. My hobbies include genealogy and refinishing furniture. My husband is a rural mail carrier."

Speaking of her AQS show experience, Elsie says, "Making the quilt was an exercise in patience: I'm a hurry-up and get it done person. It was really a challenge to slow

down and do a good job. Winning encouraged me to try again – gave me more confidence, though I still have a long way to go. Perhaps unfortunately, once you've won a competition, some people see you as an expert and (1) expect every piece of work to be equally fantastic and (2) think you have all the answers. I guess that, while I enjoy being 'famous,' at the same time, I don't want people to treat me any differently or see me as set apart from others because of it. I find conflict within myself."

Elsie gives other quiltmakers the same advice she frequently gives herself: "Don't be discouraged by rejection or not winning – keep trying. Study other winners (and non-winners) to see what makes them special. Talk to other quilters. Be realistic in your evaluation of your work. There's a tendency for us to let emotional involvement cloud our judgment in many areas of life, including quilting."

"Every time I take AMISH EASTER BASKETS out and look at it, it's like seeing an old friend again."

AMISH EASTER
BASKETS
84" x 110"
1987
Elsie
Vredenburg

Museum of AQS Collection

Diane Edgar, Chesterfield, Missouri
Joyce Kassner, Lake Geneva, Wisconsin
Toni Smith, Belton, Missouri

Spring Fling

Speaking about the development of this group quilt, Joyce Kassner says, "Diane and I tend to have similar tastes. We met several times to determine what we wanted in the quilt, discussing what it was going to look like in the end. She did the actual drawing of the design, making everything to scale." Joyce adds, "I love doing original patterns. I can't draw, but am fortunate enough to have friends like Diane Edgar who can."

first place

1988 AQS Show & Contest Group/Team

Further discussing the origin of the design, Joyce explains, "I had been asked to teach an advanced applique workshop in St. Louis. Diane came up with the bouquet pattern for me to use in that workshop. A year and a half later, we completed the design by including the borders, carrying the hexagon part out a ways and then making it a rectangle."

The applique in this quilt was done by hand. Part of the piecing was also done by hand, and part by machine. Joyce adds, "We used a light and a dark value of four or five different colors, placing all on a green background. Most of the fabrics were from my collection as we had determined right from the start that this quilt would be mine."

About the group's collaborative efforts, Joyce says, "Diane and I have been friends for long time. We met in our first quilting class in about 1980 and have belonged to the same quilting club for years. Until I moved recently, we saw each other regularly. It was easy for us to begin quilting together." Joyce says she does more traditional patterns on her own, but the people with whom she makes collaborative quilts like to design original work. Joyce comments: "I have been fortunate enough to be able to share the creation of an original quilt with them.

"Toni Smith is an excellent quilter who sometimes follows patterns I have developed, but at other times develops her own patterns." Joyce adds, "I don't think that Diane and Toni have ever met."

Asked how she feels about the quilt now, Joyce says, "If anything, I'm more possessive now than when we won the award. I'll probably not make another one like this." Joyce adds, "I have since been working for a bank and the quilt has been on display in its foyer. Everybody who sees it loves it, which makes me value it even more." Joyce adds, "I turned down a great deal of money offered for the quilt. I don't make quilts for sale, and this is one of the pieces I could never part with."

Joyce's advice to other quiltmakers is: "If you have any interest at all in quilting, give it a try. Don't give up."

Joyce Kassner comments, "I've always enjoyed seeing how my work compares with that of my peers. I'm not in shows for awards, but to see how my quilts stack up with other people's."

SPRING FLING
90" x 101"
1987
Diane Edgar
Joyce Kassner
& Toni Smith

Joyce Murrin, East Marion, New York
Jean Evans, Medina, Ohio

Baskets, Baskets

"We enjoy making baskets and are gardeners as well as quiltmakers," explain Joyce Murrin and Jean Evans, "so the 1988 AQS Show theme just gave us 'now' impetus, and we thoroughly enjoyed designing this quilt."   .

second place

1988 AQS Show & Contest Group/Team

Twins Joyce and Jean learned to sew garments at early ages but did not quilt together until 1985, when they made MAY SHADOWS, which is now part of the Museum of the American Quilter's Society's permanent collection. Joyce has developed a distinctive style in making original pieced quilts without using the traditional block setting format. Her award-winning quilts are often seen in exhibitions throughout the country and in publications. Jean divides her time between teaching art and designing and constructing art quilts. Her figurative applique pieces employ large shapes, simple gestures, many patterns and surface embellishments. BASKETS, BASKETS was juried into the "Visions 1990" show.

The quilt is hand appliqued and hand quilted and several of the baskets are hand painted. The border and small areas of the design are machine pieced. Hand embroidery and *broderie perse* flowers are also included.

Asked what they would like viewers to know about their quilt, Joyce and Jean reply: "Besides the fact that it was so enjoyable to design, we would like people to take notice of the quilting design. First we quilted around the pattern pieces. Then we quilted on these shapes and out into the border using the pattern shapes and patterns on the printed fabrics. The random placement of a repeated grid on all four sides of the border maintains continuity while allowing tremendous freedom for design in all the rest of the border."

About their award and the competition these quilters say, "The most important thing in making an artistic statement is that *you* like it, and you will like it if the finished product is what you originally envisioned or were able to work out during the design, and in this case, fabric selection and construction. To have other people express interest and enjoy the work is the ultimate compliment." They add, "The award is a confirmation for us to keep working together."

To other quiltmakers, Joyce and Jean give the following advice: "PRACTICE, PRACTICE, PRACTICE. Don't be complacent. In design, venture out and do what you haven't done before. Competitions with a written critique help you assess your technical skills. Winning in competitions will happen for two reasons: technical skill with good design and luck. Remember, there is always another quilt as good as yours, somewhere."

Left: Jean Evans; Right: Joyce Murrin

"Winning an award in the AQS Show, with its very stiff competition for both entry and awards, is magical and an affirmation that two heads can sometimes be as good as one!"

BASKETS,
BASKETS
78" x 100"
©1988
Joyce Murrin
& Jean Evans

Sylvia Apple & Antoinette Holl
State College, Pennsylvania

Appalachian Spring

Describing the way they work together, quiltmakers Antoinette Holl and Sylvia Apple explain: "During the planning and construction stages, we are very focused on the details and separate aspects of the process. Once the quilt is completed it can take on a life of its own, allowing each of us and others to appreciate it as a unified whole."

third place

1988 AQS Show & Contest Group/Team

Commenting further on the development of this award-winning quilt, Antoinette and Sylvia say, "APPALACHIAN SPRING evolved from the inspiration of Aaron Copland's ballet music with the same title, and the visual beauty of the rural landscape in the northern Appalachians, where spring comes late but with great anticipation. Sylvia developed the dancing figures, drawing on her figure drawing experience and skill with

applique. Antoinette used hundreds of cotton prints and her expertise in intricate piecing to construct the multi-faceted sky and mountain-scape. The combined scene was then profusely quilted by hand and machine for a rich dimensional appearance."

These quilters add, "APPALACHIAN SPRING has provided an introduction to many people across the country, and traveled to places we may never be able to visit. This allows us to connect with a wider world."

Antoinette and Sylvia live in State College, Pennsylvania, where they met over a quilt frame more than ten years ago and eventually formed a partnership. They create quilts separately and in tandem and have received national recognition for their work. Their quilts are exhibited around the country, and their workshops and classes have introduced hundreds of people to the many joys of quiltmaking.

To other quiltmakers, Antoinette and Sylvia suggest: "Make the quilt first of all to please yourself; then any rejection won't be lasting because the piece will always be meaningful to you."

Left: Sylvia Apple; Right: Antoinette Holl

"APPALACHIAN SPRING is an original design by two people.
Working jointly to design as well as execute a quilt is a fairly
unusual way to work, but for us it has been very satisfying."

APPALACHIAN
SPRING
98" x 75"
©1988
Antoinette Holl
& Sylvia Apple

Eileen Bahring Sullivan
Columbia, South Carolina

Over, Under, Around And Thru

Eileen says of OVER, UNDER, AROUND AND THRU, "The design is original, and a further exploration in my Ribbon Series of quilts. Its purpose was a color juxtaposition experiment where each of the twenty-two colors would come in contact with every other one at some point. A 'weaving' made this possible, using one set of colors on the vertical, and the second on the horizontal.

best wall quilt

1988 AQS Show & Contest

The quilt is machine pieced from a detailed fabric mock up, and hand quilted with two lines within each ribbon. What Eileen would most like people to know about the quilt is that "it is the result of a great deal of experimentation in the *design stage*, rather than depending upon difficult or intricate piecing to achieve the desired effect. The use of "fabric mock ups" is helpful to determine whether you have achieved your goal, *before* the top is pieced. The title refers to the fact that

each ribbon goes over and under each other, then turns the corner and meets up with its counterpart (dark to light). The main verticals and horizontals are pieced through the back also, as if they were actually woven in.

Born in Connecticut, Eileen lived there until she moved to South Carolina in 1987. She completed a B.S. and fifth year in art education, and taught art at all grade levels for eight years. The first major competition she entered was in 1985, the first AQS show. She has had a piece in *every* AQS show, also winning in 1986, 1990 and 1991. Eileen adds, "AQS Shows have always been special for me, and success at

them has helped tremendously to further my career and reputation as a quilter. In addition to my work, I lecture, judge, and have recently began publishing patterns. My work has been published in many magazines, books and calendars."

About this award-winning piece, Eileen says, "I was pleased at the time, and still consider it to be one of my favorite pieces in that series. My work has moved on in other directions since then, which I have found equally exciting and rewarding."

To other quiltmakers, Eileen says, "For those interested in working with innovative design, it is crucial to have full command over technical basics, without which even the *best* design will produce a quilt which will not stand up to stiff competition. Often we see great ideas poorly handled, which is unfortunate, and a disappointment to all. For purposes of growth, both artistically and technically, smaller pieces give you more opportunities to learn without the time commitment required by full-size quilts."

"It adds validity to one's work when it is well received in major competition, and tends to make you challenge yourself to do as well with the next piece."

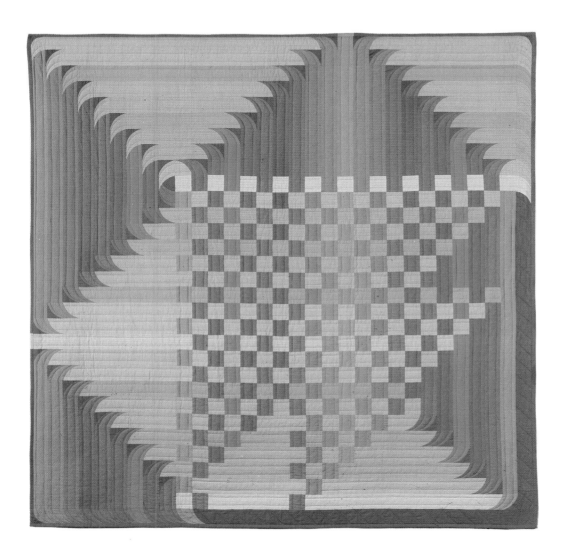

OVER, UNDER,
AROUND
AND THRU
62" x 62"
©1988
Eileen Bahring
Sullivan

Marguerite Malwitz
Brookfield, Connecticut

Desert Dusk

Marguerite Malwitz comments, "After working on beach-related themes for a number of years, several wonderful trips to the Arizona desert inspired me to change focus. DESERT DUSK was my first Southwest quilt. It was built around the original design of a three-leaf prickly pear cactus plant set in a desert landscape."

first place

1988 AQS Show & Contest Wall Quilt, Ama

Materials used in the quilt included cotton, cotton blend, tie-dyed, satin, and silk fabrics, along with cotton and metallic quilting threads. For the most part, the quilt was machine pieced and hand quilted.

Marguerite explains how the quilt was constructed: "The cactus leaves were made from five groups of fabrics, representing the light to dark color changes in a sunset. Strip-pieced cactus leaves were then positioned on the work wall, and the desert background area was filled in by working up and over from the bottom left-hand corner."

Speaking of the quilting, Marguerite explains, "I used colored quilt lines in the desert background to indicate distance. The horizontal lines in the foreground are wavy and spaced out. As these horizontal lines move up the quilt, they straighten out and become closer and closer together. A copper-colored metallic quilting thread was used in the cactus leaves and shows up nicely on the back of the quilt. The reverse side of this quilt represents the

Photo: Don Cousey, Staff Photographer, *Waterbury Republican*

desert night, simply highlighting the distant dark mesa and night sky in several specially chosen purple fabrics."

Marguerite's background includes a degree in art education and several years teaching public school art. Marguerite comments, "Following teaching jobs and while my boys were young, I was a weaver executing large tapestry commissions, doing this for about 18 years. In 1986 I switched gears and began exploring quiltmaking as an art form." Her quilts have won many awards, including ones in AQS shows and the "Memories of Childhood" contest. Her quilts have also been included in Quilt National shows and in "Visions 1990." Her work has also been featured in publications, she has written articles and she presents both lectures and workshops. She adds, "Aside from family time with my husband and two boys, I am happiest when alone in my studio, working on my quilts."

Considering DESERT DUSK, Marguerite comments, "Looking at my use of color, I

"I still like DESERT DUSK several years after making it. I continue to feel very strongly about the integrity of this particular quilt block. It is a good block and worthy of further exploration and use."

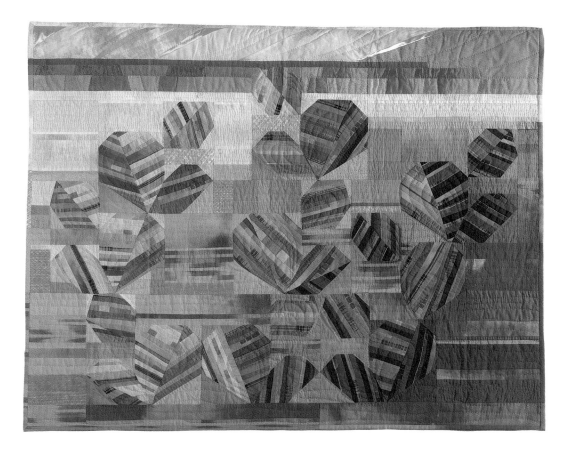

DESERT DUSK
53" x 43"
©1988
Marguerite
Malwitz

feel that my approach was conservative and subdued in comparison with my work today. It is good to look at this or any one of my quilts against the total lot of my work and see that there has been growth."

About her award, Marguerite says, "Adding to the list of accomplishments a first place in the AQS Amateur Wall Quilt category attracted the attention of groups contacting speakers and workshops. I also found a win like this was a real positive stroke of encouragement that said 'your work is good; keep making quilts.'"

Marguerite advises those interested in making original art quilts: "Set goals, objectives you want to accomplish in one year or two to five years. Put your efforts in these directions and learn to say 'no' to even good opportunities that take you away from your goals. Make studio time a priority. Go at your quiltmaking as a 'job.' Work hard to develop your own unique style. Have each quilt you make be a growing and challenging experience."

Jan Grose
Columbus, Indiana

Corridors of Color

Jan Grose says the block pattern used in this award-winning quilt is a variation on the traditional Attic Window block. This variation was one submitted by a child for "Quilt Expressions '87," a contest sponsored by the *Indianapolis Star*.

second place

1988 AQS Show & Contest Wall Quilt, Ama

The quilt is machine pieced, of 100% cotton fabric, with a small amount of applique used. Jan adds, "It is hand quilted with lots of straight-line quilting. Quilter's quarter-inch masking tape really helped."

Jan is an elementary school counselor and has been quilting about fifteen years. She belongs to the

Columbus Star Quilters group, and especially likes to "use old patterns and develop their graphic qualities in contemporary settings."

Speaking of her quilt's award, Jan says, "This was my first competition quilt. Winning this award was a tremendous thrill and a great deal of fun for me and the members of my quilt group, who were able to share the event with me."

To other quiltmakers, Jan suggests, "The work you do should add to the joy in your life rather than add to its stress. Learn to appreciate your accomplishments and don't waste time worrying that your work may not be perfect."

"CORRIDORS OF COLOR is still my favorite quilt.
I have completed very little since then, as I have little time
to quilt. I would like to create a new favorite quilt."

CORRIDORS
OF COLOR
40" x 46"
1987
Jan Grose

Joy Baaklini
Austin, Texas

Milky Way Brocade

Speaking of the development of MILKY WAY BROCADE, Joy Baaklini comments, "I was influenced by an 1890's quilt pictured in *Kentucky Quilts*. The block design is a Night & Noon variation with a pinwheel for the center."

third place

1988 AQS Show & Contest Wall Quilt, Ama

Joy received a BFA in 1974 from the University of Texas at Austin, and pursued photography as a hobby until 1983. She explains, "After the birth of my first child I became more home-bound, and with that, quilting also entered my life. I have been exhibiting quilts since 1986 and have been very fortunate to have won awards locally and nationally and had most of my work published. The rewards and awards have been more than I ever dreamed. I have a very modest studio in my home, and hope to contribute to the healthy growth of this marvelous medium by exploring the blending of old and new. Quilting has developed a new aesthetic which I celebrate."

About MILKY WAY BROCADE, Joy says, "This quilt was made from hand painted two-inch squares which were pieced into six-inch blocks. The hard edge painting was achieved using masking tape and opalescent fabric paint. The quilt is machine pieced and mostly machine quilted."

Joy explains further, "When mixing the paint I only mixed enough color to paint a few shapes, and then I would mix more on the palette for a few more shapes. Using this approach, I could never

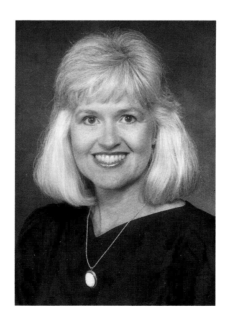

duplicate exactly any color, but I achieved many, many subtle color variations. In this way I feel this quilt is an especially honest, direct outflow of my creativity. The fabric manipulation in this quilt created a rich, opulent surface for the eye, just as brocade is to the hand.

"MILKY WAY BROCADE was my first art quilt. Its now my favorite quilt, though I didn't realize it would remain so when it was first completed. It just gets better and better. I never tire of looking at it. The contrast between the hard edges of the geometrics with the fluid waving lines which overlay the subtle patterns of the printed fabrics is an endless fascination to my eye.

"Making this quilt made me want to dust off my BFA and really pursue making quilts as an artist. For me quilting, whether the approach be traditional, contemporary or as 'art,' is a genuine medium to express the abstract, interpret the personal, or manipulate the formal elements of art. So my best advice to other quiltmakers is to listen to their own voice, amplify it

"I think I have come full circle, from quilter to artist to quilter. We are lucky in this time to witness this quilting rebirth, growth and recognition into an artistic medium so accommodating it can encompass artists from many other mediums."

MILKY WAY
BROCADE
52" x 52"
1987
Joy Baaklini

by making and showing as many quilts as possible. And to be sure to take judging with a grain of salt, unless the ribbon is on your quilt! In other words, better have a good sense of humor, good sense of self and a lot of determination. Competition is tough. It can never seem 'fair' to everyone, but it's a fantastic motivator."

Carol H. Gersen
Boonsboro, Maryland

Rivers In The Sky

This award-winning quilt is based on the Log Cabin block, used in a Streak of Lightning set. Speaking of the quilt's design, Carol H. Gersen comments, "I am sure I was influenced by four of my previous quilts made in 1986, which all used vertical zigzags in their composition."

The top was machine-pieced of 100% cotton fabrics hand-dyed with fiber-reactive dyes. The quilt was then hand quilted, including the signature and date in the lower left corner.

first place

*1988 AQS Show & Contest
Wall Quilt, Pro*

Of her background, Carol says, "I received a B.F.A. degree from Moore College of Art and Design, Philadelphia, PA, in 1969. I worked as a corporate interior designer in Philadelphia for eight years, and started making quilts when my husband, our daughter and I moved to rural Maine in 1977. My dedication to this art form began in earnest after I attended a workshop taught by Nancy Halpern. I later attended a Jan Myers-Newbury workshop on fabric dyeing. My work consists of pieced studio art quilts often based on traditional American patchwork patterns. Using simple shapes and designs allows color and value to dominate my work. Since 1986, I have gradually converted to using only my hand-dyed fabric in my quilts because of its unlimited color range and superior light fastness."

Asked what she would like people to know about this quilt, Carol says, "It is a large quilt, and I think this scale is important to the success of the piece. Although this is a studio art quilt, its size and pattern harken back to its folk art predecessors. The gradation of color made possible by new techniques and dyes is also essential in creating the blending of the vertical zigzags in the middle of the piece and in the border."

Commenting on her award, Carol says, "Using the money to contribute to the furnishing of a new house gave me a feeling of having a high enough professional standing to use my income for non-quilt expenses; i.e., showing a profit."

To other quiltmakers, Carol says, "Improper lighting can severely damage your quilt. There should be no natural (outside) light of any kind. This includes skylights. If windows are present, they should be covered completely. Fluorescent lighting which contains ultraviolet light is also very damaging. The overall light level should be about fifteen footcandles. Don't be afraid to ask about lighting at exhibits because many groups are simply unaware of the possibility of textiles fading while hanging, and many insurance policies are cleverly worded to avoid claims related to fading."

*"RIVERS IN THE SKY was the first big quilt that I made
with fabric I had dyed with fiber-reactive dyes.
Its selection as a winner affirmed this direction in my work."*

RIVERS IN THE
SKY
72" x 72"
©1987
Carol H.
Gersen

Helen Kelley
Minneapolis, Minnesota

The Unicorn Quilt

"THE UNICORN QUILT," says Helen Kelley, "is a quilter's version of a *milles-fleurs* tapestry. Each appliqued creature, each tree, each embroidered plant is a Renaissance symbol for a virtue. The unicorn is a very specific one, from the Unicorn Tapestries in the Cluny museum. The mother and child are my daughter, Faith and her son, James, kneeling beneath the Cross of St. James."

second place

1988 AQS Show & Contest Wall Quilt, Pro

Helen continues, "This is really two quilts in one. The background is entirely pieced in miniature flowers. The flowers have been redrafted on three-eighths-inch squares and triangles rather than diamond shapes to facilitate machine piecing. Every spray

of flowers is different."

Summarizing the experience of making this quilt, Helen says, "This brings together my love of Renaissance art, enjoyment of rich color, and affection for a new grandchild. How could I possibly have made another, different quilt?"

Helen has been a quiltmaker for much of her life. A 1972 photo article in the Minneapolis *Sunday Tribune*

introduced her work to the public. Since then, she has been actively teaching and lecturing around the world. She is also a magazine columnist and the author of two books: *Scarlet Ribbons, An American Indian Technique for Today's Quilters*, and *Guidelines for Dating Quilts*.

Asked if she feels any differently about this quilt now than when she completed it for the show, Helen says, "I look back on this quilt and I still love it. I loved making it. But I am ready to move on to something different."

Asked to give advice to quiltmakers who enter competitions, Helen says, "I have asked the judges in three large shows what they especially saw in the Sweepstakes quilt. Three different judges in three different places said exactly these words – 'It was flawless.' So, I guess it has to be a combination of 'knock-your-socks-off' beauty, and perfection."

"I won't be blasé and pretend otherwise – winning in a quilt show is a thrill. You keep going back to look at your quilt with its ribbon, just to be sure it's true."

THE UNICORN
QUILT
46" x 60"
©1987
Helen Kelley

Karen Maguire
Lisle, Illinois

Winter Daffodils

Karen Maguire explains that WINTER DAFFODILS is original in design and was made in response to an event in her life: "This quilt was made as an expression of the joy I've felt when, in the midst of winter here in Illinois, I've received a box of fresh-cut daffodils from my elderly grandmother who lives in northern California. Every February she sends me this gift of spring."

third place

1988 AQS Show & Contest Wall Quilt, Pro

The quilt is constructed of 100% cotton muslin which Karen has hand-dyed and then strip pieced by machine, and string quilted. Speaking of her background, Karen says, "Inspired by the work of Jan Myers-Newbury, I have been hand-dyeing fabric

and making original design quilts since 1985. Quilting has recently taken a back seat to my 'other' life as a student. I am currently pursuing a master's degree in social work."

Asked about the effect of participation in the AQS competition and winning an award, Karen says, "I am pleased that others liked WINTER DAFFODILS, and that the pleasure I took in making this quilt was visually imparted to others."

Asked to give advice to other quiltmakers, Karen says: "Don't take rejection of your quilt as rejection of yourself. Keep entering other competitions. Other judges may judge it differently. Keep trying!"

Asked if she feels any differently about WINTER DAFFODILS now than when she first completed the quilt, Karen Maguire says, "Yes. I find its value to me increases over time."

WINTER
DAFFODILS
38" x 63"
©1988
Karen Maguire

Anne J. Oliver
Alexandria, Virginia

Parrots In Paradise

The applique and quilting designs in PARROTS IN PARADISE are original. Anne J. Oliver explains, "The quilt is whole-cloth, one piece of 90" wide muslin with no seams. The appliques were made with freezer paper folding, and the six-foot-long border applique is continuous. The appliques are open, so reverse applique stitching was applied in the applique 'holes.' Symmetrical, asymmetrical and random quilting designs are incorporated,

viewer's choice

1988 AQS Show & Contest

showing that all can be mixed effectively. My children's names were quilted into the background in Hawaiian. The quilt is fun."

Anne adds, "I was seeing how big an applique I could make with freezer paper. The six foot border was the result. I discovered something else during this project: you need to very carefully watch the fabric you use in your work. I was careful, but apparently not careful enough. A big flaw in the muslin top got by me. I had to cover a hibiscus quilting pattern with a patch. "

Anne began quilting in 1975. She explains, "I made every mistake in the books, but finished my first quilt and became addicted. I chose to lecture, give workshops, etc. instead of taking a full-time job when my children began to grow up. I was a frustrated oil painter and watercolorist, but quilting became the expression of my love for art." Anne has published articles, and is now interested in presenting architectural motifs in her quilts, "bringing back the metal ceiling era at the turn of the century."

Speaking of PARROTS IN PARADISE, Anne says, "The quilt has not found its home yet; when it does, I will be able to say goodbye to it."

About the competition, Anne says, "The AQS Show creates a quilting goal for me. I would easily put down the work and never finish if goals were not established. Those goals have to be enough incentive for me to put 1,200 hours into a work and want to finish when my fingers are crying 'no, we've had enough.' "

Anne is especially pleased with the award she won at the 1988 AQS Show. "The Viewer's Choice award is my most special. I treasure it so much that I find it's a great boost when I am a bit burned out or disappointed. But, just putting your quilt into an AQS show is prestige enough; you will gain more self-esteem through that than through anything else you do."

"As I develop quilts, I experiment with how much freedom a quilter has in creating the quilt top and the designs used for quilting. I've discovered the answer is – lots, lots, lots."

PARROTS IN
PARADISE
92" x 92"
1986
Anne J. Oliver

Eleanor J. Carlson
Cadillac, Michigan

Cinderella

Speaking of the development of her quilt, Eleanor J. Carlson says, "Although I did all the work on CINDERELLA, people's ideas were jewels to grasp and I was wise enough in my ignorance that I knew I needed the help from whatever place it came." She explains that she "had no pattern for it, but got ideas from many sources: magazines, coloring books, other books." She adds, "I feel the Lord gave me the idea and the influences, as they came from many places and people."

first quilt award

1988 AQS Show & Contest

Eleanor "had never made a picture quilt before." She adds that she learned much in the course of her work, including how to use a small needle and a thimble and how to applique using a six-inch embroidery hoop.

Eleanor comments further: "When I was still working on it, the Lord impressed upon me I hadn't made this quilt myself. He gave me the talent but used other people as well as me to make the finished quilt. This Lord is in heaven, the doors are about to open, the midnight hour has struck. He will come in all His Glory, the angels with Him. We will be changed; the animals will all be our friends; the earth will be changed. We will be taken in an instant, our work buckets and brooms left. Have your lamps lit. The wicked will be cast into outer darkness, the stars in heaven will fall. God's

love never ends, like my border, a continuous cable. He has no beginning or end."

Speaking of the AQS award her quilt won, Eleanor adds, "I feel it's God-given – his tangible gift to me to show and show to all. He choose me to do this, too. Even though it won Best of Show at Dollywood and the prize was a substantial purchase award, I waived my right to accept the award and chose to keep the quilt so I can freely talk to people at churches or groups and tell and show them this story. It inspires all who see it."

The competition has had an effect on Eleanor. She explains, "I now feel that if I take my time to do my best, I can come up with one-of-a-kind quilts and use all the talent that lay dormant over the years to produce quilts of beauty for all to see and enjoy." It has also had a second important effect. Eleanor says, "I can also tell my story about this quilt; before I was scared to talk in a small group setting."

*Eleanor says to other quiltmakers, "Use the talent
God has given each of you and improve it. "*

CINDERELLA
74" x 88"
1988
Eleanor J.
Carlson

Quilt Show & Contest

1989

The fifth American Quilter's Society Quilt Show & Contest was held April 20 through 23, 1989, at the Executive Inn Riverfront in Paducah, Kentucky.

Judges for the quilt show were Patricia Morris, Glassboro, NJ; Katie Pasquini Masopust, Oxnard, CA; Mary Coyne Penders, Vienna, VA.

Category award sponsors were as follows:

Best of Show, American Quilter's Society
Gingher Award for Workmanship, Gingher, Inc.
First Quilt Award, Great American Quilt Factory
Traditional Pieced, Amateur, Hobbs Bonded Fibers

Traditional Pieced, Professional, Coats & Clark
Innovative Pieced, Amateur, Fairfield Processing Corp.
Innovative Pieced, Professional, Concord Home Sewing
Applique, Amateur, V.I.P. Fabrics
Applique, Professional, Mountain Mist
Other Techniques, Amateur/Professional, Viking/White
Theme: Circles, Amateur/Professional, That Patchwork Place
Group, Amateur/Professional, Wrights/Swiss-Metrosene, Inc.
Best Wall Quilt, RJR Fashion Fabrics
Wall Quilt, Amateur, Silver Dollar City
Wall Quilt, Professional, Fiskars
Pictorial Wall Quilt, Amateur/Professional, Pfaff American Sales Corp.
Viewer's Choice, American Quilter's Society

In each category three awards were made: 1st place, $800; 2nd place, $550; 3rd place, $300. The Gingher Award for Excellence of Workmanship was a $3,750 award; the Best of Show Award, $10,000; the Best Wall Quilt Award, $2,500; and the First Quilt Award $500.

The exhibit included over 400 quilts, representing 50 states and Australia, Canada, Germany, Holland, Israel, Japan and Switzerland. Viewers attending were asked to select their favorite quilt, and a Viewer's Choice Award was made after the show.

The second block contest was also held during this show, along with the third quilted fashion contest sponsored by Hobbs Bonded Fibers. New in 1989 was a non-competitive exhibit of kites. And, once again, the entire city of Paducah celebrated quilters and quiltmaking with special events.

Caryl Bryer Fallert
Oswego, Illinois

Corona II: Solar Eclipse

Speaking of her inspiration, Caryl Bryer Fallert says, "I can remember seeing a movie about the solar eclipse when I was a young child in grade school. I particularly remember the pictures of powerful solar 'storms' flaring hundreds of miles out into the sky from the corona of the sun. These images inspired this quilt.

best of show

1989 AQS Show & Contest

"This is my second quilt portraying a solar eclipse, the moon coming between the earth and the sun so that the disk of the sun is covered. The corona is the envelope of ionized gasses surrounding the sun's chromasphere, which is visible during a solar eclipse.

"Both the front and back of the quilt were constructed using a string piecing technique in which strips of fabric are sewn directly to a full size drawing of the finished design. The quilt is constructed of 100% cotton fabrics, dyed and over-dyed in both chromatic and value gradations, which create the illusion of movement and light on the surface of the quilt. The top and back were machine quilted together in a design that spirals out from the center of the disk of the moon to the edge of the sky and into the borders."

About her development of the quilt, Caryl says, "I had been thinking about making this quilt for a year and a half before I started it. When I found out the last week of December that I had a thirty day leave of absence from my job in January of 1989, I decided that this was the

time to do the quilt. Fortunately, all of my mental, physical, and creative energy came together at that time."

"I only had CORONA II: SOLAR ECLIPSE for two weeks after the last stitch went in, before it was shipped off to the AQS show. When the Museum of the American Quilter's Society opened in April 1991, I saw it for the first time in two years. It was like visiting an old friend, and I was delighted by the beautiful way in which it was displayed and lighted."

Speaking of her award, Caryl comments: "Winning the AQS Best of Show Award was one of the biggest thrills of my life. It has led to a number of invitations to exhibit my work, and to teach and lecture. It also led to several publications including an astronomy magazine, where it illustrated an article about an historic solar eclipse in China, and the covers for a musical group's cassette, CD, and songbook titled *Fire Within*."

To others, Caryl says, "Always follow your heart. If your head and your heart disagree, follow your heart!"

"CORONA II: SOLAR ECLIPSE is probably the best quilt I have done to date. I have completed approximately 50 quilts since I completed CORONA, but I don't think any of them has been better. I'm still trying to top it."

CORONA II:
SOLAR ECLIPSE
76" x 94"
1989
Caryl Bryer
Fallert

Museum of AQS Collection

Janice R. Streeter
Virginia Beach, Virginia

Spring Flower Basket

The original design for this stunning quilt was adapted from the traditional basket pattern. Janice explains, "Since my first encounter with prairie points, I have loved them and anything else that provided texture. One of my favorite traditional patterns is the Star Flower because of the gathered petals. A discussion with a friend about basket quilts

gingher award

for workmanship
1989 AQS Show & Contest

brought these three 'loves' together in this quilt. The corded-wreath alternate block was designed to coordinate with the texture of the pieced and appliqued blocks."

Three years in the making, this quilt is constructed of 100% cotton unbleached muslin, blue and burgundy prints and solids, combined with a bonded polyester batting. The quilt includes "pieced and appliqued baskets with prairie points and strips forming the baskets and gathered, stuffed petals

forming the flowers. It is quilted in an overall basket weave design with vines and flowers along the border."

About her quiltmaking, Janice says, "Since my mother was an avid quilter, I was surrounded by quilts throughout my childhood. I had no interest in them, however, until 1977. At that time I received a large box from my mother, which contained three quilts, one for each of my children. As I took them from the box, I was so struck by their beauty that I immediately decided to try my hand at making one. Since I

have never been taught to quilt, my methods are somewhat unorthodox."

Asked how she feels about this award-winning quilt, Janice replies, "I loved it from the moment of conception and enjoyed every minute spent working on it. In fact, I am now working on another basket quilt along the same lines, but with a new twist."

She adds, "It has been personally gratifying to create this quilt and to have it recognized for excellence in workmanship by way of the AQS Gingher Workmanship Award and the NQA Master Quilter's Guild Program. I am delighted this quilt is now in the Museum of the American Quilter's Society, where it can be shared with and enjoyed by many, many people."

To other quiltmakers, Janice says: "Let your imagination run wild. Try new ideas and techniques and improve upon them if you can. Entering competitions gives you the opportunity to see where your skills can be improved and also the opportunity to share your work with other quilters."

"To me, the quilting is one of the most important parts of a quilt because it brings everything together and provides texture."

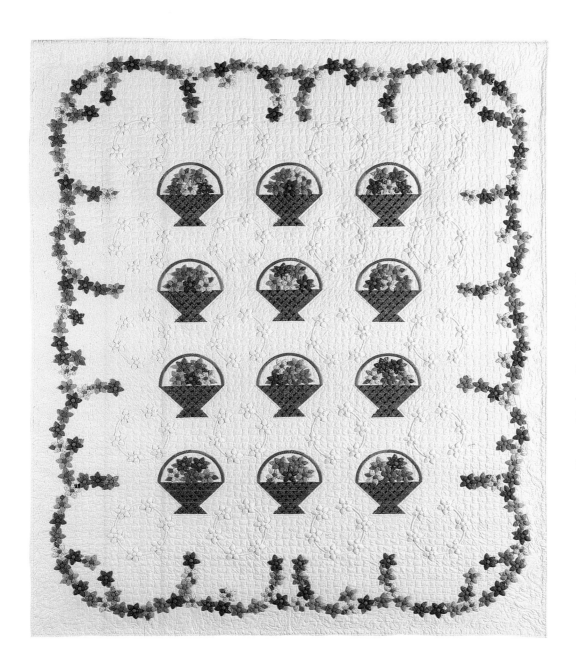

SPRING
FLOWER
BASKET
88" x 103"
©1984
Janice R.
Streeter

Museum of AQS Collection

Beverley Cosby
Mechanicsville, Virginia

Frank's Star

Beverley Cosby's inspiration for this outstanding quilt was "a picture of an antique quilt and a fabric – the floral Jinny Beyer print." She adds, "Often I will see a fabric and like it so much that I will try to come up with a design to use it effectively." The right design in this case was a star with eight very sharp points, dramatically set with plain blocks.

first place

1989 AQS Show & Contest Traditional Pieced, Ama

Beverley explains that the quilt was constructed completely of 100% cotton fabrics, and was totally hand pieced and hand quilted. She adds that it was "not made from blocks, but rather was pieced in strips as explained in *American Quilter* magazine, Fall 1989." She adds: "I liked the quilt very much during all stages of construction, as well as the finished product. I have made several since this one but still feel it is my best, although not necessarily my favorite."

Beverley has been married 34 years, has one son, an 'adopted' daughter-in-law, and two grandchildren, and works full time as a legal secretary. Of her quilting, she says she has "done all types of handwork, knitting, embroidery, etc., but gave them all up for quilting about 1976 or 1977," when she made her first quilt from a kit. She adds, "My main hobby 'BQ' (before quilting) was flying my Cessna™ 150 three or four times a week."

Asked about her award, Beverley explains, "Winning an award, especially this one involving a large monetary award, seems to make non-quilters have more respect and appreciation for the

quilts I have made. They are not looked upon as 'just blankets' anymore, an attitude which, I must admit, irritated me to no end! Winning this award was also a great boost to my ego and now I am inclined to be a little less traditional in my thinking when considering my designs and also those of other people that I see. Of course attending the show twice probably had a lot to do with my change in attitude, too."

To other quiltmakers, Beverley says: "When you get an idea or see a design you would really like to make but feel you will not be able to do it, try anyway. I have begun projects and had no idea how I would construct them. They did not always work out on the first or even the second try, but eventually something would occur to me. FRANK'S STAR is a good example. I tried several methods before coming up with the idea of strips. Blocks just would not work because too many points would have come together at one place to get the star points really sharp. I believe the strips were try number three!"

"I feel quilts 'speak' for themselves. They are what they are and what the individual sees in them. I think that is one thing so fascinating about most antique quilts – our conclusions as to who might have made them, why and how."

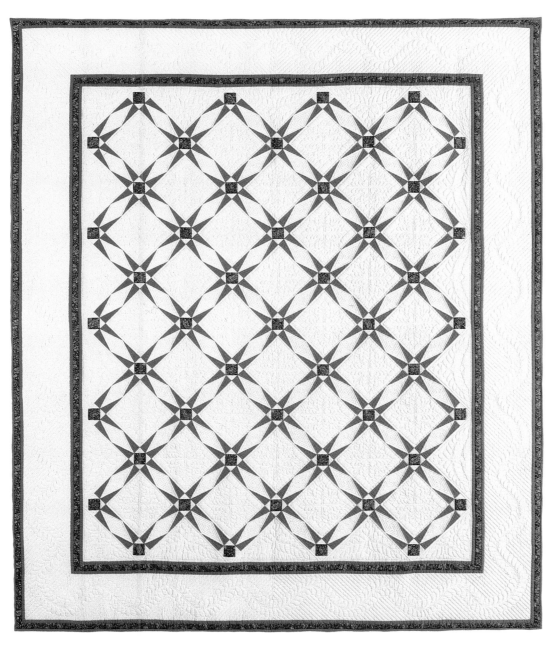

FRANK'S STAR
83" x 99"
1987
Beverley Cosby

Jeanne Tanamachi
Lauderdale, Minnesota

Dresden Baskets

Jeanne Tanamachi explains, "The block pattern in this quilt is a combination of the Parquet Basket and a Dresden Plate, set in a red and green sashing. Each block is the same, and all of the fabrics used are 100% cotton, including a printed muslin and two border prints. The top was hand and machine pieced, and then hand quilted."

second place

1989 AQS Show & Contest
Traditional Pieced, Ama

Jeanne adds, "This is the most traditional quilt I have ever made. While I like it very much, I do not feel that it says much about the way I like to make quilts. I now know that I prefer to use a wide variety of fabrics in most quilts."

A lifelong resident of Minnesota, Jeanne holds a B.A. in American history, with some additional coursework in library science. She explains, "After nearly 20 years in the paid workforce, I decided to stay at home after the birth of my second child. This allowed me some time to develop my interest in quilts. Now that my daughters are school age, I work and teach at a quilt shop in St. Paul, volunteer in the school library, and pursue the art and craft of quiltmaking."

Speaking of the development of this award-winning quilt, Jeanne comments, "I cannot forget that I developed a troublesome case of tendonitis in my elbow while rushing to get this quilt ready for a show; it was a lesson in the value of moderation."

She continues, "The award I won for DRESDEN BASKETS was the second time I'd won an AQS award. (The first time was in 1987, when my quilt took the third prize award in Traditional Pieced, Amateur.) It meant that many people decided I was 'for real' as an accomplished quiltmaker. Because of some opportunities that came my way after the second award, I will no longer be competing in the Amateur class; I'm a professional now."

Asked for her advice for other quiltmakers, Jeanne simply says, "You can't enter your quilt if you don't finish it. You can't win a prize if you don't enter."

"If everyone were reluctant to enter quilt shows, we would not have very interesting shows. Remember that each of the other entrants is taking a chance, too."

DRESDEN
BASKETS
73" x 92"
1988
Jeanne
Tanamachi

Mary Jo McCabe
Davenport, Iowa

The City Surrounded

Mary Jo McCabe explains that the center design of this quilt was inspired by Jinny Beyer's INNER CITY quilt, and its block based on the hexagon. She points out that the Baby Block border is also based on a hexagon.

This quilt, which has won ten ribbons, is constructed of 100% cotton fabrics and was hand pieced and hand quilted. Mary Jo adds, "All pieces were cut so that the grain line was running the same direction. I feel this is the main reason that the quilt hangs straight."

third place

1989 AQS Show & Contest Traditional Pieced, Ama

Speaking of her background, Mary Jo comments, "I began quilting in 1979, and I'm basically self-taught. I've progressed from traditional, repeat-block, two-color quilts, to quilts using many fabrics and innovative designs. Quilting, for me, has been the ultimate hobby. It has eased the transition from being a busy mother of five to being 'home alone,' and allowed me to create in fabric and color."

Asked if she feels any differently about her quilt now than when she completed it, Mary Jo says, "No. I liked this quilt while I was making it. It was fun to work with all the different fabrics. It is still one of my favorite quilts."

The award has had positive effects on Mary Jo. She explains, "It has given me more confidence in my ability to make quilts. I have since been asked to do a number of quilt programs in the area, and more people know me as quilter."

Her advice to other quiltmakers is: "Strive for perfection and innovation. Entering competitions is a marvelous way to have your work evaluated. I've learned from every judge's comment."

"With each new quilt, there is a new challenge, and I am constantly learning."

THE CITY
SURROUNDED
74" x 91"
1988
Mary Jo
McCabe

Hanne Vibeke de Koning-Stapel
Bilthoven, Holland

Stella Antigua

"This quilt," explains Hanne Vibeke de Koning-Stapel, "is a memory of a sailing trip in the Caribbean. Our youngest son sailed the Atlantic Ocean and we joined him in Antigua. On this trip I started piecing the Lone Star part. It was meant as an octagonal tablecloth, but my husband didn't like it on the table. So it went into the cupboard. After some months I thought out how to make a bed quilt out of it, and he likes it now."

first place

1989 AQS Show & Contest
Traditional Pieced, Pro

Hanne Vibeke says, "The pattern is based on 45-degree diamonds creating a variation of the Lone Star in the center and Virginia Stars in the broad borders and corners. I wanted the applique border because I had many irregularly shaped pieces of fabric, and because I love old traditional quilts that combine piecework and applique."

"The materials," says Hanne Vibeke, "are all silks. A small piece of Liberty® silk was the inspiration for the colors. The silks have very thin Vlieseline® (fusible non-woven interfacing) ironed to their backs. Marianne Fons' book *Fine Feathers* inspired the quilt patterns and helped me draw my own patterns."

Hanne Vibeke lived in the U.S.A. in 1973 and 1974 and was fascinated by the quilts she saw in friends' houses. In 1978 she met an American, Sophie Campbell, living and teaching quilting in Paris. Hanne Vibeke took classes with her in Paris and in Holland, and in 1981 she

attended the West Coast Quilters' Conference, where she learned much. Back home she started teaching classes.

About her award-winning quilt, Hanne Vibeke says, "It now lies on the bed in our guest room and it is still a nice memory of our sailing trip. In addition it's now also a very nice memory of the exciting days during the 5th Annual AQS Quilt Show, where it surprisingly turned out to be a winner."

Speaking of her award, Hanne Vibeke says, "The attention afterwards in the Dutch quilt world and a write-up in a leading Dutch ladies' magazine were other important benefits. I am now regularly working for this ladies' magazine, and it gives me great satisfaction to reach readers who don't know anything or don't know very much about patchwork and quilting."

Her advice to others is advice she was once given: "An American teacher once told me: 'What is worth doing, is worth doing well.' Often I convey this message to my students – it is so simple and so true."

"It's important to be open to other people's (not necessarily just quilters') advice and critiques, but it's more important to listen to your inner voice and follow your own judgement in the end."

STELLA
ANTIGUA
91" x 91"
1988
Hanne Vibeke
de Koning-
Stapel

Edith Zimmer
San Diego, California

Victorian Lilies

Edith Zimmer comments, "Most of my quilts start as scrap quilts. I then coordinate the background and border to the quilt blocks. The blocks in this particular quilt are the traditional Carolina Lily pattern. Scraps of border prints were used for baskets and calyxes."

second place

1989 AQS Show & Contest
Traditional Pieced, Pro

She continues, "The border is my original design and is made using a technique I have developed. The border was constructed by overlapping the border fabric onto the quilt and top stitching the desired design, trimming off excess fabric and covering the stitching with contrasting Celtic trim. I call this process my 'Sculptured Border.' "

Speaking of her background, Edith says, "I have been sewing all my life for myself and my family. I did not get into quilting, however, until the mid-1980's, hanging my first quilts in the San Diego Quilt Show in 1986. I have taught quilting in San Diego area quilt shops for the last three years." She adds, "I sell many of my quilts and generally do so with no regrets as I feel I have derived my enjoyment from the process of making

the quilt. I find, however, that the longer a quilt is in my possession, the more attached to it I become."

Describing her AQS show experience, Edith comments, "I design and make my quilts in the solitude of my sewing room, so I do not experience any feedback during the process. I work with great excitement and compulsiveness. It is extremely encouraging when the reaction from either the general public or judges is positive. My award at the AQS show has brought my quilts recognition and brought me many new friends. It has given me much encouragement to do better and to try new things."

Edith gives the following advice to others: "Make your quilts to please you! Enter your quilts in shows and know that many other quilters will truly enjoy your efforts, and the feedback that results will help you in your creative growth!"

"Generally I do not share my quilts with anyone, even my best friends, until they are completed, so it is with great anticipation that I enter my quilts in shows."

VICTORIAN
LILIES
69" x 86"
1988
Edith Zimmer

Betty Patty
Bradford, Ohio

Oklahoma Dogwood

Betty Patty says about this award winner, "This quilt is based on a pattern from Mountain Mist™ batting company with a pieced dogwood blossom appliqued onto a background. I later filled the quilt with Floral Scroll and Dogwood quilting patterns. Made in soft mauves and soft greens, it is an all-cotton quilt, including cotton batting."

third place

1989 AQS Show & Contest Traditional Pieced, Pro

She continues, "I enjoyed the challenge of using existing floral quilt patterns and combining them with some of my own original designs. The selection of colors also offered me a challenge because I had never hand dyed materials before."

Betty was "born into a large family on a farm in Miami County, Ohio." She adds, "I am part of the country and farm life. Married over 50 years to Dale Patty, an area farmer, I began making quilts in 1977 for my family – two sons, grandchildren, nieces and nephews. I'm also active in church, grange, and social activities, and I enjoy cooking and growing roses."

The first thing Betty says when asked about her award is, "I never expected to win,

even though my 1985 entry had been purchased for the Museum of the American Quilter's Society's permanent collection." She adds, "The award boosted my confidence and encouraged me to rediscover what I'd done to create a winner!"

The award has had an effect on Betty's life. She explains, "It has encouraged me to continue competing with my quilts. I've been included in every AQS show entered. Also, I've been asked to give talks and presentations, been invited to judge local competitions, and been asked to share ideas with local quilt groups. My winning helps others see that success is actually attainable, and encourages them to explore their own creativity."

Betty encourages other quilters to "find a good club or teacher rather than just start out alone and learn through trial and error. It will save a lot of 'mistake' time."

"I'd encourage even beginners to enter contests. I have learned more from that than any other way! The judge's comments are very valuable!"

OKLAHOMA
DOGWOOD
78" x 86"
1988
Betty Patty

Kitty Pippen
Lake Almanor Peninsula, California

Cranes

"Growing up in the mountains of rural China with Chinese playmates and no television, radio, supermarkets, or department stores has certainly influenced my values," says Kitty Pippen. "My appreciation of fine needlework comes from

first place

1989 AQS Show & Contest
Innovative Pieced, Ama

watching Chinese women do cross stitch, mend and quilt their padded garments, and decorate the toes of baby shoes with little tiger faces. After coming to America, there followed college, teaching school, raising a family, and retirement. Now I live on a beautiful lake with Mt. Lassen in view. Watercolors and counted thread embroidery are on the back burner, for I have discovered the wonderful world of quilting!"

Kitty explains, "This quilt is an innovative pattern with Oriental designs. A piece of Japanese kasuri cloth depicting two mirror-image cranes inspired the central theme, and ideas for sashiko came from family crests and traditional Japanese designs."

Japanese yukata cotton was used for the cranes and border, and even the curved shapes were machine pieced. Sashiko quilting done with #8 pearl cotton stitched through all three layers

embellishes the surface. Background quilting on the indigo was done with a different pattern in each quarter. Quilting on the yukata was innovative, based on the design of the fabric

"When the quilt finally came together," Kitty comments, "I was happy and excited. I felt really inspired. But though I felt CRANES was a good piece of work, I never dreamed it would win a first place award at AQS, nor did I ever imagine what doors would open for me: teaching workshops, lectures, quilt shows and, best of all, making many new friends."

Kitty comments, "Along the way I have been trying to educate myself about Japanese fabrics and explore new ways to use them in quilts." Her advice to others is: "Make a quilt that pleases you. Then, don't hesitate to enter competition, if for no other reason than to see how your creation compares with other people's."

"I hope CRANES won't be the first or last success I have as a quilter. It has sort of taken on a life of its own. The ribbons and prizes are won by 'it' and not by me!"

CRANES
100" x 100"
1988
Kitty Pippen

Lita Star
Franklin Square, New York

Square Dance

"Basically, this quilt is a one-inch Postage Stamp pattern," says maker Lita Star. She then adds, "Of course, that is an oversimplification. Native American designs and Amish quilts are strong influences in my work."

Lita continues, "The quilt is made from all cotton materials. The piecing had to be fairly innovative because it is not made in traditional quilt squares, and is all machine pieced, except for one small section that had to be hand appliqued."

second place

1989 AQS Show & Contest Innovative Pieced, Ama

About her background, Lita says, "Although I have been sewing most of my life, I only found quilting about six years ago, and it was as though I had finally found what I had been searching for. I trained for and worked as a chemist many years ago, have three grown sons, three

lovely daughters-in-law and five grandchildren. I have designed and made special quilts for each grandchild, and everyone else in the family is waiting in line because I work very slowly. I must add that my husband is very patient and understanding and loves it when I hand quilt during football season so he has company watching televised games."

Asked to comment on her AQS Show experience, Lita says, "How fortunate I am that with my second large quilt I was able to take a

prize at Paducah." She continues, "At this stage in my life, it has given me a tremendous lift and confidence in my ability to be someone more than my sons' mother or my grandchildrens' grandma – to have my own identity. However, the awards for this quilt and also my first large quilt have made me a little bit nervous about whether my future work can live up to these standards." She adds, "When I have finished a quilt and come back to look at it a year later, I wonder if I will ever be able to do it again, make the color decisions, design the quilt pattern. Then, suddenly, thoughts come together for a new design and I am immersed again."

To others, Lita says: "First, you must please yourself with the design, color and workmanship. Being accepted into a show or winning in a competition is additional compensation – but you are still the best and the severest judge of what you create."

"A quilt takes a great deal of time and effort. It is something you make because you really want to."

SQUARE
DANCE
83" x 99"
1989
Lita Star

Martha Jane Muth
Plainfield, New Jersey

Rose Window of Notre Dame

Martha Jane Muth explains that this quilt is developed from an "original block" which is "repeated with rotational symmetry." She explains further, "The graduated color range was influenced by a rose window at Notre Dame Cathedral in Paris, France."

third place

1989 AQS Show & Contest
Innovative Pieced, Ama

She continues, "Raw silk noil was selected for its intensity of color. Each piece of silk was cut on its proper grain orientation so that the entire quilt hangs straight with no sagging. Outline quilting is used to emphasize the block design." A wool batt was used, the lanolin content of which Martha says made it easy to quilt.

Born in Woodbury, NJ, Martha received a B.A. in fine arts from Douglass College and an M.F.A. in drawing and painting from Rutgers University. She has been employed as an art teacher since 1978.

Asked what she might like

others to know about this quilt and her quilting, Martha says, "Having made a quilt which was painstakingly symmetrical, it is understandable that I sought a more free-form construction in my next quilt." She adds, "I commend the efforts of AQS in recognizing and promoting the quilt as a viable fine art medium of expression."

Giving advice to other quiltmakers, Martha says: "Never make an art quilt specifically for a competition or for a specific theme. It will always have an element of contrivance. To the experienced eye and heart, the quilt will always have an inauthentic quality, an unfelt color, shape or tone. A quilt takes its own sweet/difficult time to be made. It cannot be rushed to completion for the sake of a deadline alone."

"Make a quilt because your whole being cries out for it to be made."

ROSE WINDOW
OF
NOTRE DAME
72" x 92"
©1988
Martha Jane
Muth

Wendy Richardson
Brooklyn Park, Minnesota

Fragmented View: Northern Nights

Speaking of the development of the design for this original quilt, Wendy Richardson explains, "The pattern I began with was the Pinwheel. I varied the rectangles I drew these Pinwheels in, and then assigned visual images to various parts of the pattern – stars, sky, trees, etc. I eventually decided to put these blocks in windows, floating over a landscape."

first place

*1989 AQS Show & Contest
Innovative Pieced, Pro*

Wendy continues, "FRAGMENTED VIEW: NORTHERN NIGHTS is constructed from cotton fabrics, some dyed, some over-dyed. It was impossible to find the right blues without dyeing my own. Some of my grandmother's scraps were also included. She, too, was a quilter. The quilt is hand pieced and hand quilted with patterns which relate to the images on the quilt."

Wendy still feels the same way about her quilt as she did when she first completed it, but the award has affected her life. She comments, "After winning once, and especially after winning twice, a big change is that everyone suddenly asks you what you're going to do next. I like the challenge of entering, but cannot accept those outside pressures because to me the quilts are strictly a personal challenge to my creative expression. The awards are just icing on the cake!"

Wendy Richardson's advice to other quiltmakers is: "Just do it!"

FRAGMENTED
VIEW:
NORTHERN
NIGHTS
66" x 88"
©1989
Wendy
Richardson

Patty Hawkins
Lyons, Colorado

5.5 On The Richter Scale

Speaking of her background, Patty Hawkins says, "I came to quilting six years ago from fifteen years of watercolor, though I had always sewn and loved fabric. Quilting offers a much larger canvas, and purchased fabrics give me a wonderful variety of color and texture with which to work. I find myself completely consumed by quilting."

The original design for 5.5 ON THE RICHTER SCALE, Patty explains, "evolved from drawing one block and working with it in various sequences to accomplish the optimum visual patterning

second place

1989 AQS Show & Contest Innovative Pieced, Pro

with respect to blocks neighboring each other." Patty had taken a class with Nancy Crow, who emphasized the necessity of establishing shapes which will have visual dominance in a composition. This quilt was the first Patty created "deliberately concentrating on the

positive/negative aspects."

"5.5 ON THE RICHTER SCALE, as so often happens," says Patty, "contained surprises after I got all the fabric on the pin wall. The multiple play of shapes, foreground, and background seemed quite successful, again due to predetermining which shapes I wanted to be dominant and subordinate. Though everyone calls this THE WATERMELON QUILT because of one print, it was always 5.5 ON THE RICHTER SCALE to me, because I created it right after the devastatingly horrific earthquake in Azerbaydzhan, Russia,

and the patterning represented the markings on the Richter scale. I also worked to utilize the leftover blocks in a surprise for the back of the quilt; for the hard working people who hang quilts for shows."

Patty says awards such as the AQS award are "encouraging to an artist." She explains, "It always feels good to have the work you enjoy be appreciated by others, after having worked on it in the solitude of the studio. This was particularly gratifying, as many people do not understand contemporary quilting, but we all feel compelled to be creative in this wonderfully tactile medium."

To other quilters, Patty says: "Do what you enjoy best, keep working in one direction, become tunnel visioned, focused to fine tune your craft, your awareness of composition and your awareness of play of colors and pattern against each other."

Patty adds, "Constantly train your eye; constantly draw, to continue your own style. GO FOR IT! Work hard daily, or it won't happen."

"With grown kids and my husband totally encouraging me, I can devote all my time and energies to quilting. The only problem is, we quilters need to live to be 184 to accomplish all the quilts we conjure in our heads."

5.5 ON THE
RICHTER
SCALE
66" x 86"
©1989
Patty Hawkins

Lyn Peare Sandberg
Capitola, California

Boats In A Bottle Sampler

"The boat pattern," says Lyn Peare Sandberg, "was designed by my friend Joyce Lund, as a block of the month quilt project (©Bonnie Leman, 1991). The block appealed to me because it seemed to have a windward motion. Having just finished an entire landscape using J. Schlotzhauer's curved piecing method, I naturally thought of rounding the corners and adding a neck to produce a boat in a bottle.

third place

1989 AQS Show & Contest Innovative Pieced, Pro

My husband is a boatbuilder and model maker at heart." Lyn adds, "Making this quilt relieved my repressed sailing energy when my husband dry docked our sailing dinghy for the entire season."

Lyn explains that her fabrics were carefully chosen: "I used fabrics with tropical and water motifs, wood grains and neutrals to construct the boats, and abstracts to convey transparency and atmosphere –

offset madras, starry ginghams, windswept prints, sky dyed." The quilt is machine pieced and hand quilted in bronze cotton thread, in original and Japanese motifs.

Born in Kodiak, Alaska, Lyn was raised in California and taught quilting at the age of eight by her aunts. After college she settled in a small beach community on Monterey Bay where she cooked professionally, sailed, and eventually became a custom seamstress. Lyn continues telling about her background, "In the early eighties, I progressed, with the financial support of my husband and

the artistic support of my local quilting guild, to dealing exclusively with quilts – producing my own pieces, commissions, restorations, and more recently vintage replicas and also becoming involved in appraisals, designing and publishing."

About her quilt, Lyn says, "I've always been pleasantly surprised at its initial and continuing success, now becoming a pattern for sale by Bonnie Leman Publications. I have always thought the quilt should hang in a substantial building like a bank or library.

"Entering and winning my first national competition at AQS has given me answers about my work that only showing at a national level can do. It encouraged me to focus on pattern innovation, and the recognition it afforded me also opened doors in the designing and publishing world."

To other quiltmakers, Lyn says, "Preserve your artistic integrity and motivation by making quilts for yourself rather than for competition purposes, or for someone else's tastes."

"I would like to be able to share the beautiful bronze quilting which molds and gilds this quilt. Unfortunately, it doesn't seem to reproduce well in publishing. I always wonder what I'm missing in pictures of other people's quilts."

BOATS IN
A BOTTLE
SAMPLER
80" x 92"
©1989
Lyn Peare
Sandberg

Museum of AQS Collection

Louise Young
Tioga, Pennsylvania

Silversword – Degener's Dream

Louise Young explains that this quilt is Hawaiian in design and was made by modifying an Elizabeth Akana (EA) pattern. The fabric and batting are 100% cotton. The backing fabric is a fine cotton floral fabric, printed in Hawaii.

About its construction, Louise says, "While I was making this quilt, I tried to follow all of the quiltmaking traditions from Hawaii."

first place

*1989 AQS Show & Contest
Applique, Amateur*

Louise used the traditional Hawaiian method, the needle-turn applique technique, and the quilting is in ¼" echoes on both background and pattern fabric. Teal and gray metallic threads were used to give the appearance of sunlight off water. Louise says of her experience, "I was amazed at how much I felt like an Hawaiian by the time I finished the quilt! This quilt has changed my outlook on quilting – I no longer feel I have to do everything in pre-

cise, straight lines. I have developed a more flowing, free attitude."

Speaking of her background, Louise explains, "I have been quilting since 1972. I'm self-taught, and have averaged a quilt a year since then. People who know me from other places can't believe I make quilts because I am a very physically active and 'outdoorsy' person. My hobbies include canoeing, cross-country skiing, mid-

distance (3-16 miles) race running, and hiking. Every summer, I spend two weeks on a solo wilderness backpacking trip in Montana, so the passing years for me are measured by the making of my annual quilt and the taking of my annual backpacking trip!"

Louise adds, "I have a master's degree in botany, specializing in ecology, so nature and especially plants are very important in my life. Most of my quilts are based on images from the plant world."

Louise comments, "This quilt and the AQS award have enabled me to 'come out of the closet.' I was always a little embarrassed by my quilting – it seemed like a rather strange thing for an active, thirty-something woman to do. The AQS recognition and the other awards I have received for this quilt have enabled me to admit to people 'I make quilts,' without hesitation (usually!)."

To others, Louise says, "Make quilts to satisfy yourself! You are the ultimate judge of your work, so if you are satisfied with your work,

"The silversword plant is endemic to the lava fields of the Hawaiian Islands, and it is listed on the international endangered species list. The title of this quilt also honors Otto Degener, a botanist who has worked to catalog and preserve the native flora of Hawaii."

SILVERSWORD – DEGENER'S DREAM
97" x 97"
©1988
Louise Young

Museum of AQS Collection

don't listen to anyone else who comments on the color, pattern, etc. Everyone has different tastes and you'll never please everyone, so try to please only one person – yourself!"

Adabelle Dremann
Princeton, Illinois

Country School

Adabelle Dremann explains that the original design used in this quilt was first drawn on 9" x 12" paper. Then sections were enlarged to full size, and used as patterns. She adds, "I am influenced by Grant Wood's paintings, but do not copy them."

second place

1989 AQS Show & Contest
Applique, Amateur

The quilt is made of all-cotton quilt percale. Some of the pieces are Jinny Beyer fabrics. The quilt was entirely hand quilted, using a 22" round hoop.

Asked about her background, Adabelle says, "One of my favorite childhood pastimes was drawing pictures with a pencil and making doll clothes. In 1929 I received a two-year certificate in art education from Illinois State University at Normal and taught art in elementary schools until I married. I spent the next 45 years on a farm. My first two quilts were a double bed size and a baby crib size. Night quilting was done by the light of a kerosene lamp, on the lap hoop that I still use for my quilts today."

Adabelle continues, "Then quilting was laid aside for many years. In 1957 I returned to teaching, and was dabbling with oil paints. Upon retiring from teaching in 1973, I joined the St. Matthews Quilters, a local church group that does custom quilting. I have learned much by working on the quilts of others, seeing first-hand the fine ones, the mistakes and pitfalls, the various materials used."

She continues, "In 1985 I

started to make original pictorial quilts. The years grow shorter now, but they are full of many rewarding memories, and hopefully a few more quilts, too."

Asked if she feels any differently about COUNTRY SCHOOL now than when she completed it, Adabelle replies, "I don't think so. It is very hard for me to part with my quilts. I used to paint pictures, which I did not mind parting with, because I had not put as much time into them."

Commenting on her competition experience, Adabelle says, "The award was one of my life's biggest thrills, and locally, my small and brief claim to fame. It inspired me to start another and continue as long as I can do it well. The two most enjoyable parts were thinking up the design and the AQS show. In between was tedium."

To other quiltmakers, Adabelle says, "Attend shows, to learn by looking. Then strive to make more even stitches, perfect the applique or piecing, and just be very accurate and particular. I can't do a quilt up fast."

"My quilts are sort of a daydream put down with pieces of cloth."

COUNTRY
SCHOOL
73" x 92"
1988
Adabelle
Dremann

Museum of AQS Collection

Juanita Whiting
Woodstock, Illinois

Birds In A Rose Tree

Juanita Whiting explains, "BIRDS IN A ROSE TREE was made when my son Brad was married. I wanted to carry on the tradition of giving a quilt as a gift. I had never had any left to me, as none of my ancestors quilted." She continues, "This was my first appliqued quilt. I tested myself to do the best I knew how, and this quilt turned out to be far more than I had anticipated when I started the first block."

third place

1989 AQS Show & Contest Applique, Amateur

The quilt involves an adaptation of two old patterns: "the Rose Tree or Prairie Rose applique patterns with vines, birds, grapes, and leaves on the borders." Juanita adds, "What I'd read about this type of quilt was that they were used as wedding quilts. This was my gift to my son for his wedding in April 1989."

The quilt is constructed of cottons and is hand appliqued and hand quilted.

Juanita comments, "The birds are quilted two-by-two, with feather wreaths, feathers radiating from the center with straight lines, feathers outlining the vine border, and a one-inch square grid overall. There is ⅛" red piping just inside the binding."

Juanita says of her background, "I have been married to Jim for thirty years, and we have three sons. I worked in design for fifteen years, and then left to pursue my hobby of sewing. I found quilting in 1987 through a sampler class, and I am now teaching applique with some machine work."

About her award-winning quilt, Juanita says, "I look at my accomplishment and know that I can just about do what I want if I set my mind to it. I feel joy and jubilation when I see it."

She adds that the award has had positive effects on her life: "I am now teaching and people respect my input. It also gave me the insight to improve my work in the technical aspects as well as the artistic aspects of the craft. I had never entered a contest before.

"I know I'll enter again; the feelings of winning and being accepted are such rewards for having done something for someone else."

To others, Juanita says: "Don't be afraid to try something that is beyond your skill level – you may be surprised and pleased with the results." She continues, "Competition is fun and a wonderful learning experience. You meet many people with the same interests as you. The critique sheet is good for knowing where you shine and also where you need to improve. If in doubt – 'Just Do It.' "

"My son and daughter-in-law are so proud of this quilt that the time it took to make it seems like a short span, even though it took me an entire year."

BIRDS IN A
ROSE TREE
95" x 95"
1989
Juanita Whiting

Velda E. Newman
Nevada City, California

Hydrangea

Speaking of the development of this original design, Velda E. Newman says, "With this quilt I wanted to try to portray a bird's-eye view of hydrangeas, to put the viewer right there. I dyed a wide range of blues and lavenders and did stipple quilting in contrasting thread to add texture."

first place

1989 AQS Show & Contest Applique, Pro

"The most important element in my work," says Velda, "is color – it's what catches your eye and draws you in for a closer look. I use all-cotton fabrics, and if I can't find just the right color or value, I dye the fabric or use a controlled bleaching technique. Dyeing and bleaching give me a wider, richer range of colors to use for my designs."

Continuing to discuss her quilting, Velda says, "Once I've designed a quilt on paper, I cut and pin full-size fabric pieces to my wall board. When I'm satisfied with their placement, I baste and begin the applique. I use many pieces in multiple layers and keep my stitches very close."

Velda quilts her works in "a freehand motion that follows the contours of the applique." She explains, "I see quilting as another design tool that enhances the overall look of the quilt."

Velda was an art major in college, and has sewn since she was a child. She began making traditional pieced patterns about eight years ago, but quickly discovered she did not like matching points. She was soon appliqueing, and developing her own patterns. She comments, "My work is large. I always mean to make smaller quilts, but most become about seven by eight feet. I put in approximately one thousand hours on each one and plan to spend twelve months on a project." She adds that her latest quilt "is a still-life composed of pears, grapes, and leaves, in purples, greens and golds."

"I love flowers, and most of my quilt compositions are taken from nature. I gather ideas from gardens, magazines, and photos."

HYDRANGEA
100" x 97"
1989
Velda E.
Newman

June Culvey
Garden Prairie, Illinois

Colored Nectar

June Culvey explains that the patchwork, applique and embroidery in this award-winning quilt are of her own design, with the exception of the hummingbirds, designed by Carolyn and Wilma Johnson for Old World Designs™.

The quilt is medallion style, with appliqued feather gradations, and is made with a combination of hand-dyed

second place

1989 AQS Show & Contest
Applique, Pro

solids and 100% cotton calicos. June adds that the quilt "was not made to represent a color wheel." She explains, "I simply used the colors of hand-dyed fabric I had on hand. For instance, there is no true red represented – I didn't have any! I just wanted to somehow use the fabric in feather gradations."

Continuing to discuss the quilt, June adds, "It was fun to do; working with a lot of colors is easier for me to do. The quilt I just finished had only two colors plus brown.

What a pain it was to do."

June adds, "I never plan a quilt – I just let it develop as I go. I use a very crude method of pattern making. The outside curves of COLORED NECTAR were drawn on old wallpaper and cut. I'm always surprised when the pieces actually fit together. The hardest part was choosing the black/gray background. I needed something dramatic to set off all the colors. I hope I achieved that."

June quilted the quilt by hand in gray thread, in a large Hinterberg frame. For her outstanding quiltmaking and quilting skills, she

received her Master Quilter designation during 1991 with TRANQUIL VIOLETS. It was nominated by the Master Quilt Judges of the National Quilting Association.

Speaking of shows and competitions, June says, "I have a very small work area (a dining room) to do my quilts in. From start to finish I'm eyeball to eyeball with them. I can never stand back and see how things mix. When my quilts are in shows, I finally get to see them at a distance. The first time a quilt goes to a show is a very nerve-wracking time for me – not because I'm worried about winning or losing, but simply because I will finally see whether the quilt 'works' or not."

She continues, "It is very important to me that quilt shows hang my quilts full out with dignity, not draped or scrunched or used as a decorator piece on a chair or another piece of furniture. The American Quilter's Society is one of the most dignified shows we have, and I'm very pleased with how they handle my quilts."

"COLORED NECTAR kept me sane going through some tough times with our children. As usual, 'things have a way of working out' with kids and quilts. The pieces get put together and come out pretty decent if you stick with it. "

COLORED
NECTAR
96" x 98"
1989
June Culvey

June recommends: "Allow your quilts to be shown in good quilt shows. Don't be afraid to send them, carefully packaged and properly insured. Remember the people receiving them are usually quilters, so they know how to handle them. Refusing to display your quilts only deprives the rest of us from seeing something unique."

Anne J. Oliver
Alexandria, Virginia

Painted Metal Ceiling

Anne Oliver explains, "This quilt was influenced by a salesman's book of ceiling tiles from about 1900. I converted ceiling plates to quilt patterns and presented a quilt in the ceiling style." Anne adds, "This was all done with freezer paper. My goal is to get freezer paper out of the kitchen and into the sewing room!"

third place

1989 AQS Show & Contest Applique, Pro

One hundred percent cotton was used, and reverse appliques were created with a shading of beiges to accentuate the appliques. The quilt is one piece of fabric, so no piecing was necessary. An extra-loft batt allowed the designs to "pooch," so no stuffing was necessary.

Anne started quilting in the mid 1970's, and she now gives workshops and lectures and writes articles for magazines. She encourages quilters to enter shows to gain confidence, etc. Anne adds, "This quilt was the third in the metal ceiling series and the most rewarding. It carried whole-cloth white work a step further because toned beiges were added to give the designs more highlights, yet all appliques were quilted inside and out, as though they weren't there."

Anne adds, "The quilt was far more photogenic than all my previous white quilts. How many people have said, 'White work looks like mattress covers.' This quilt helps dispel such disparaging remarks. Because of its unusual construction, it is remembered far longer than most of my work. All the designs (appliques and quilt designs) were done with freezer paper, my ally and constant companion."

"I treasure this quilt," says Anne, "but I could say goodbye to it if I were to sell it. It belongs on a far bigger wall than I would want, and it should be treated as a piece of art. It almost stopped my desire to attempt other work. I did not want to create another of its kind. It's hard to go beyond it. Still, the interest in it, the techniques I worked on to finish it, have been transferred to a new piece of work. How many memories about metal ceilings it has brought forth from viewers at shows. Perhaps it will help revive interest in them!"

Speaking of the series, Anne says, "Hazel Carter encouraged me to create the metal ceiling series. I had felt I did not want to do more than one quilt about any one subject. To do three and enjoy each one more than its previous creation shows that a quilter's interest can create an effective series and keep boredom from setting in. As to a fourth, I don't think so, but Hazel is still around looking over my shoulder."

About quilt shows, Anne says: "AQS and other quilt shows have always been my goals for finishing my work." She continues, "The monetary awards are wonderful, but those dogwood ribbons last a lot longer than the money one receives. The next time you look at the prize winners in a show, look at their ribbons, too. Enough can't be said about them."

Anne says, "I encourage quilters to enter shows, all kinds." She adds, "Please

*"PAINTED METAL CEILING has opened so many new avenues for me,
and traveled more places than any other quilt I've made.
It has also had fan mail letters addressed to the maker of it."*

PAINTED
METAL CEILING
80" x 80"
1988
Anne Oliver

think twice before deciding not to put that finished piece in a show, whether it is judged or unjudged. People's entering quilts is what allows us to have shows and enjoy the camaraderie they create."

Debra Wagner
Hutchinson, Minnesota

Winter Bouquet

Debra Wagner says, "This quilt was inspired by the fragment of a circa 1860 quilt that had survived a house fire." Continuing, she adds, "It is a white work quilt designed in four quarters, each quarter featuring a vase and flowers. There is also an undulating feather border, and a large floral border outside of that."

first place

1989 AQS Show & Contest
Other Techniques

The quilt is made of 108" wide Range Finder™ cotton, front and back, and Debra split a Cotton Classic™ batting for the filler. Speaking of the quilting, Debra says, "The quilt is entirely machine quilted, with a stippled ground. Every space on the quilt is trapuntoed."

Debra holds a B.S. in clothing, textiles and design from the University of Wisconsin/Stout, and has been a machine embroiderer for over twenty years. Her interest in machine work is not surprising – her parents have been

Bernina™ sewing machine dealers for twenty-five years. Debra has taught machine techniques for fifteen years, and her embroideries have appeared in national competitions and publications. In 1987 Debra became interested in machine quilting and piecing because of her "love of antique textiles." She adds, "My favorite quilts have challenging piecing or applique, with lots of quilting and trapunto. I am a traditionalist in design, if not in technique." Debra's quilts have won many awards and been featured in publications.

Asked if she feels differently now about WINTER BOUQUET than when she first made it, Debra says, "Yes. I've forgotten much of the grief and boredom that is an intrinsic part of making a large white quilt. Also, I've become more blasé about its beauty." She explains, "When it was first completed I was shocked to realize it had turned out so well, and I was as nervous as a new mom about letting it out of my sight or letting anyone touch it. Now, it spends months in storage, and is packed and unpacked as it travels with me when I teach."

About the effect of her AQS award, Debra says, "Winning has brought a new

"My main areas of interest are cutwork, lacemaking, and developing machine techniques that give the appearance of traditional handmade textiles, but require a fraction of the time and effort."

WINTER
BOUQUET
90" x 95"
1988
Debra Wagner

career into my life. I am a professional quilter, author, and pattern designer. The best part of the career is being able to make quilts. If I were a homemaker, I could not keep making quilts just to try out a design or prove to myself I could master a pattern. With it being my career, someone pays me to have fun!"

To other quiltmakers, Debra says, "Do something you love. A truly good quilt reflects the spirit of the maker. Enter competitions. But, take the outcome of competition with grace, whether you win or lose. A single quilt is a fraction of our worth; winning doesn't make us better people any more than losing makes us worse."

Beverly Mannisto Williams
Cadillac, Michigan

Amish Spring With Feathers And Lace

Beverly Mannisto Williams comments, "I appreciate all quilts, but enjoy best working with the whole-cloth style. This pastel Amish-style Diamond in a Square is as close as one can get to a playground for quilting."

second place

1989 AQS Show & Contest
Other Techniques

"I have been a seamstress and craft person for as far back as I can remember," says Beverly. "I had been bothered for many years that we are a throw-away society; I was ready to make projects which would be longer lasting, to be appreciated by future generations. This naturally and happily led me to quilting and bobbin lacemaking. Just as I cannot imagine life without my family, I cannot imagine life without the great satisfaction I receive through these crafts. I enjoy needlework that draws you in for a closer look at the intricacy of workmanship, which stirs your emotions for the appreciation of the creator."

Beverly adds, "I have been most fortunate that my quilts and their bobbin lace have won numerous awards, including prestigious awards through AQS, NQA and AIQA."

Speaking of the development of AMISH SPRING WITH FEATHERS AND LACE, Beverly says, "The quilt designs were lightly traced with a #2½ pencil from a pattern beneath the 100% cotton." Most of the designs were original. Beverly comments, "Never finding intricate feathered plume patterns to my satisfaction has led to designing most of my own quilting motifs." Beverly quilted with a 12" hoop, using no thimble, and then enhanced the motifs with trapunto. On the quilt she also showcased a three-inch-wide edging of handmade bobbin

lace based on a Danish pattern. Beverly comments, "I have spent about 2500 hours on the quilt and 325 hours on the lace over a 15-month period. The most difficult part of the quilt for me was in lining up the background crosshatching."

Beverly continues, "I enjoy the long process needed for each quilt and lace piece. Upon completion I feel an emptiness until a new project is underway. When my 11-yard lace piece was finished, I found a more appropriate pattern and made another 11-yard piece. Workmanship is a top priority with each project I create." She adds, "When sharing an award-winning quilt with friends, I often share one of my first quilts. This allows them to know that I did not wake up one day knowing how to quilt – that at one time I, too, was a beginner."

Looking back at the award-winning quilt, Beverly says, "With this second major quilt I seem to have developed a style of my own, which I now see as a reflection of my quiet personality. My anticipation of each year's

"I look back on each quilt for possible improvements but there does come a time when you must leave well enough alone and quit nagging at them. My anticipation is always that the next one WILL be perfect!"

AMISH SPRING
WITH
FEATHERS
AND LACE
91" x 91"
©1989
Beverly
Mannisto
Williams

AQS Show, which I have been fortunate to attend since 1987, is like that felt by a child looking forward to Christmas. All of the wonderful quilts are truly gifts from their creators' hearts and hands. What a privilege it is to be involved with these special people."

Beverly says to other quiltmakers, "Put your own ideas into each of your quilts so that we as late twentieth-century quiltmakers will be looked upon by future generations as having developed our own styles."

Louise B. Stafford
Bremerton, Washington

Hearts And Feathers

Louise B. Stafford describes herself as "an 82-year-old who learned quilting back in the Midwest, from making scrap quilts at age 19." She adds, "I still have two of those quilts." She was born on a Kansas farm and later moved to Topeka, where she and her twin sister were educated. They are both avid quilters, and though Louise had moved to Washington by the time she and her sister started quilting again, they still have been able help each other out. Louise explains,

third place

*1989 AQS Show & Contest
Other Techniques*

"Kansas and Washington, by phone, are a short but expensive distance apart for my sister and me to exchange quilting ideas."

Louise says her engineer husband is a great help in her quiltmaking. She explains, "He re-designed the patterns, both the old and original ones, to make this quilt completely covered with beautiful quilt designs."

All the marking of quilting designs on the piece of white 100% cotton used for this quilt was done by Louise's husband. Speaking of the quilting, Louise comments, "My #12 needle flowed along, with no seams

to cross." She adds, "Mini prairie points were attached by hand, using a jig, a tool suggested by my husband, to make the curves accurate."

Louise says, "All who see this quilt want to make one! My husband did agree to mark two for my quilting friends, but it takes considerable time. To mark the tops, he built wooden sawhorses, removed our bedroom door, and placed our dining room table pads on it for a worktable. Pins hold the designs securely in place, and the felt side of the pads allows easy marking – always with a hard lead pencil." Louise says she would like to make another one herself, in a pastel color.

Louise feels quiltmakers should be encouraged to enter competitions. She says, "Four ladies from our quilt group have entered the AQS Show as a result of my urging them to be competitive."

"The ooh's and aah's from all my friends make me very proud. To show them the picture of the quilt featured in American Quilter *magazine as a prizewinner brings further compliments."*

HEARTS AND
FEATHERS
108" x 108"
1988
Louise B.
Stafford

Deon Spangler
Neillsville, Wisconsin

Oriental Dream

Deon Spangler explains that this original design is based on a photograph she had seen in *Modern Maturity* magazine. The photograph showed the dome in a Chinese temple located in the Forbidden City.

first place

1989 AQS Show & Contest Theme: Circles

Deon discusses the quilt's development, "It took me three months to draft the pattern and nine months to complete the quilt." Machine pieced, hand appliqued and hand quilted, the quilt contains 4000 pieces. Deon comments, "This quilt was a real challenge at every stage. It was a challenge just to draft the pattern from looking at the magazine." Deon changed the colors, but feels she captured the dome well. She explains, "I have a friend whose sister-in-law didn't know about my quilt, but happened to visit China, go into the temple depicted, and take photos. When my friend saw the photos, she said, 'That's Deon's quilt!' "

Deon adds, "This quilt was like a baby – it took nine months to make it. I still have it and I don't know if I could sell it or not."

There is not a tradition of quilting in Deon's family. Speaking of her entry into quiltmaking, she says, "I had a yarn shop and my customers persuaded me that I would love quilting. I got hooked." However, Deon adds, "I don't quilt any more. I made one more after ORIENTAL DREAM, and that was the last of any kind of quilting I did. I became completely burned out. In making this quilt I was quilting 14 hours a day. By the time I finished, I had had my fill of quilting." Deon continues, "I don't know if I will ever quilt again. I just don't know. I still admire quilts, but I haven't been to a quilt show recently, and I don't belong to any organizations or take any magazines."

Asked about the effect of her award, Deon says, "It was written up locally quite extensively, and I was invited to show my quilts. We have an old mansion that was turned into a museum, and I was invited to show my quilt there during its opening. There was a huge turnout." Deon adds, "People still talk about the quilt. I had it hanging at my church's annual statewide meeting and it received many, many positive comments. I have also hung it in my church for special occasions."

Deon sums the experience up: "It was positive even though I have never made another one." She explains, "I like challenges. After I won that award, the challenge was gone."

Asked about competitions, Deon says, "I think everybody should be encouraged to enter competitions. Whether you think you will win a prize or not, if you have created something that you are proud of, you should enter it. You can always learn something by making quilts and entering them. Nobody ever knows it all."

"Many people look at ORIENTAL DREAM and can't believe the small pieces used. Some are only a quarter inch in size."

ORIENTAL
DREAM
86" x 86"
1989
Deon Spangler

Bonnie Thornton
Redmond, Washington

Albuquerque

Speaking of her award winning quilt ALBUQUERQUE, Bonnie Thornton says, "Seeing an original design come alive as you work on it brings a great deal of fulfillment to life. It is exciting to reach inside oneself for inspiration and very rewarding when others appreciate what you have created."

second place

1989 AQS Show & Contest Theme: Circles

Bonnie explains that "the block used is an original design, as is the layout of the quilt." She adds that it was the first original square she designed after a Nancy Crow workshop.

To construct the quilt, she used cotton and cotton polyesters, solid colors and one print. She comments, "There is some strip piecing and lots of contrast of color. The quilting design was adapted from Southwest Indian pottery."

About her background Bonnie says, "I am an artist who changed from painting to quiltmaking. I have always sewed and admired the strong design of old quilts. I finally decided to try quiltmaking about thirteen years ago when the oldest of my three children was graduating from high school. I needed a new purpose in life. Now I make my own designs and pursue quilting with a passion."

Of her award Bonnie says, "I heard about winning the award for ALBUQUERQUE at a time when lots of changes were occurring in my personal life. It was a boost to my morale right when I needed it. The award offered further proof to me that I need to keep working to express myself artistically in the quilting medium."

Bonnie's advice to others: "Work to find your own voice and express original ideas."

"I liked the strength of color and design in ALBUQUERQUE when I made it, and I still do. It reflects my feelings for the place I called home for three years."

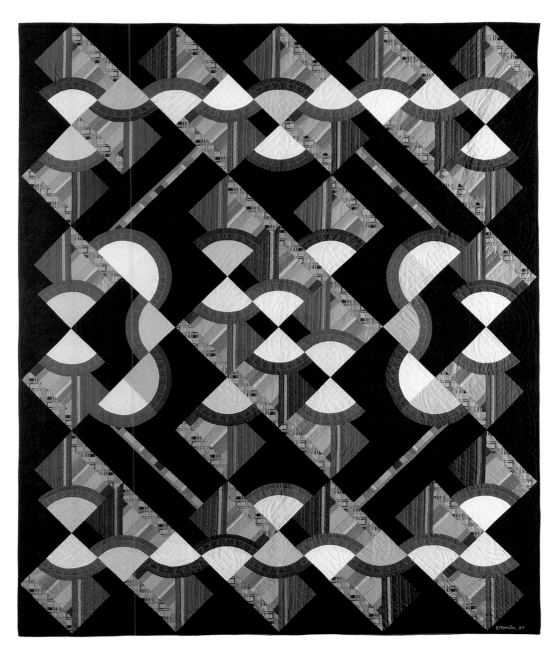

ALBUQUERQUE
83" x 101"
1987
Bonnie
Thornton

Hallie O'Kelley
Tuscaloosa, Alabama

Spheres Of Influence

"This quilt," explains Hallie O'Kelley, "relies on the basic pattern of striped overlapping circles, which I screen printed on white cotton cloth. Those near the edges of the quilt possess broader stripes than those nearer the center, which gives an illusion of transparency as one's eye moves from the edge of the quilt to the center." Hallie continues,

third place

1989 AQS Show & Contest Theme: Circles

"The quilt face is all cotton, which was either hand screen printed or dyed. The batting used is Mountain Mist™ Quilt Light®, and the piece was lap quilted by hand in segments."

Thinking of her own experiences, she adds, "I would like to recommend screen printing as a valuable technique for quilters. First of all, you can get precisely the colors you want, and second, screen printing allows for a great deal of freedom in the development of your design."

Hallie holds a Master's degree in applied art from Iowa State University, with a major in textile design. She comments, "Although I have

been sewing since I was a child (my mother taught me), I did not make a quilt until 1981." She continues, "This quilt is one of a series of pieces I have made using overlapping striped circles. Some of the others in this series are quite different."

Asked for her current feelings about this quilt, Hallie says, "When I completed this quilt, I felt it was a successful design, and I still feel that way."

About the award she won for it, Hallie says, "This was my second AQS award. It was, of course, gratifying that the judges found merit in this particular quilt. I am encouraged to continue trying new ideas and techniques in my quiltmaking." She gives similar encouragement to others, saying: "Don't be afraid to be creative and innovative in your quiltmaking."

*"All of my quilts are original designs. Typically, I start a quilt using cotton print cloth and screen print my own designs on the cloth.
I do my own dyeing to add a colored background to the prints."*

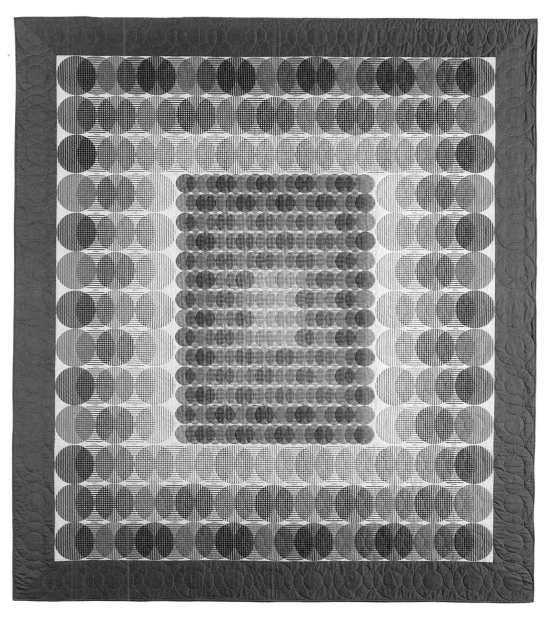

SPHERES OF
INFLUENCE
77" x 89"
©1989
Hallie O'Kelley

Chaska Heritage Quilters
Chaska, Minnesota

The Heritage Quilt

Audree Sells, director for THE HERITAGE QUILT project, explains, "There was no formal quilting group at the time this quilt was made. The Chaska Historical Society, through the *Chaska Herald* newspaper, asked for volunteers to make a commerative quilt, which would ultimately have a permanent place in the new Chaska City Hall, a building which was still in the planning stages then."

first place

1989 AQS Show & Contest
Group/Team

She continues, "The designs for this quilt are all original, created from historic photos of the town, people and events depicted. Mostly hand-dyed fabrics were used, to achieve shading and dimension, and most designs were appliqued and embroidered." She adds, "The people who came together to make this quilt had had no previous experience in pictorial quilting or applique. Over fifty people worked on the quilt in various ways and many dear and lasting friendships have been made."

Asked about the effect of the award, Audree explains, "Those with stereotyped ideas of 'quilting,' especially men, now see it as an art form and proudly escort friends and relatives from out of town to the city hall to show them our quilt on display with its ribbons. As the director of this project, the awards have resulted in requests for advice from groups around the country, speaking engagements, and the encouragement to begin our own local quilt group – the Chaska Area Quilt Club – meeting the quilter's needs in the surrounding area. Now the city of Chaska provides us with a 'quilting room' in its beautiful new Community Center which opened in the fall of 1990."

To other quilters, Audree suggests: "Be original – use your own ideas – challenge yourself. Keep the project moving – set deadlines – we selected the fabric to be used to help it all coordinate."

Audree Sells, project director: "It looked like such an impossible task when we began – we really challenged ourselves. Now everyone is proud of the quilt and takes ownership. Those who chose not to accept the challenge now wish they had."

THE HERITAGE
QUILT
76" x 86"
1989
Chaska
Heritage
Quilters

Nancy Pearson
Morton Grove, Illinois

Morning Glory

Discussing the development of MORNING GLORY, Nancy Pearson explains, "I chose a strong, bright, cobalt blue because I thought it would be the most difficult color to work with – and it was! Since I belong to a group of quilters called the Morning Glories, I automatically went to the morning glory as a source of inspiration."

second place

1989 AQS Show & Contest Group/Team

The quilt is constructed of many different cottons, with silk pieces serving as accents, and details added through embroidery embellishments." The hand quilting was completed by Ruth Bell of Wilmette, Illinois.

Nancy discusses the quilt: "Though it does contain some pieced work, this quilt is basically appliqued, with an original design I have called Morning Glory. The quilt itself is square, but most of the quilt design is actually circular. I discovered that morning glories are common to most of the Earth, so that shape seemed appropriate. There are also points in the design that represent the sun, because morning glories are at their best at sunrise."

Nancy has a graphic arts background, and she attended the School of the Art Institute of Chicago and the American Academy of Art. She became interested in quilting in 1981, and has been teaching since 1983."

Asked what effect this quilt and its award have had on her life, Nancy replies, "It has certainly given my quiltmaking some prominence. I have had many requests for teaching engagements."

Nancy's advice to other quiltmakers is: "Never make a quilt specifically for a competition. Make the quilt, giving it the best ability you have, and then enter it in the most appropriate competition. There are plenty of them to choose from."

"I think I'm typical of most quilters. I look at MORNING GLORY and think, 'There are some changes I would make....'"

MORNING
GLORY
80" x 80"
1989
Nancy Pearson

Quilted by
Ruth Bell

Sandra Heyman, Burns, Kansas
Linda Nonken, El Dorado, Kansas

Sky-Blue-Pink

Linda Nonken and Sandra Heyman have been making award-winning quilts for a number of years. They comment: "As we continue working together as a team, we are learning and growing. With every quilt or project something new pops up – exciting challenges to work through. With SKY-BLUE-PINK we set ourselves the challenge of using the same basic

third place

*1989 AQS Show & Contest
Group/Team*

grid work as for HOT STUFF (page 211 of *Award Winning Quilts and Their Makers, Vol. I*), making changes within to create another original work. Hexagons were divided, coloration was changed and the quilting design was altered to enhance the design lines."

The makers continue, "Inspiration for the quilt's name is from Sandy's grandfather's description of an early spring sunrise as 'sky-blue-pink.'

Linda was stitching the two quilt halves together before church early on Easter morning, 1988 – the sky was streaked with glorious pinks and lavenders – thus, SKY-BLUE-PINK." SKY-BLUE-PINK is paper-pieced using 100% cotton fabric for front and back.

Speaking of their backgrounds, Linda and Sandra comment: "Since winning in 1986, Sandy's son has married and she now has a new grandson. We have done four more quilts, including SKY-BLUE-PINK, and have been involved in two challenge projects. We individually are working on charm quilts and are in the process of quilting our yearly competition quilt."

Of this award, Linda and Sandra comment: "Winning this award has meant continued validation of our work. The American Quilter's Society competition is at such a high level that we are very pleased to be among the winners."

Left: Linda Nonken; Right: Sandra Heyman

"Working as a team has been a way for us to really focus on quiltmaking. We motivate each other and always have someone for encouragement and/or criticism."

SKY BLUE-PINK
90" x 102"
©1988
Sandra Heyman
& Linda Nonken

Dawn E. Amos
Rapid City, South Dakota

Looking Back On Broken Promises

Dawn E. Amos sketched her own patterns for LOOKING BACK ON BROKEN PROMISES, drawing from photographs, art magazines, and other sources. The quilt is made of 100% cotton muslin which she hand-dyed. The quilt is hand appliqued and the border machine pieced. The entire quilt is hand quilted.

best wall quilt

1989 AQS Show & Contest

For about the first ten years Dawn was involved in quiltmaking, she made star quilts, but in recent years she has been developing original designs dealing with topics she feels strongly about.

Speaking of the development of this quilt's design, Dawn says, "I try to put the viewer in the Native American's place. What are his thoughts? What is his world like? Native Americans were close to the earth, to nature. How do they relate to the environment they were forced into?" Dawn continues, "It would be nice to think that I could make some sort of impression on people, but I'm not sure explaining the quilt in words is the answer. My explanations

would take away from its effect. People bring their own experience with them when viewing the quilt, and sometimes my thoughts get in the way of their interpreting the quilt and feeling its meaning for themselves."

Asked if she feels any differently about LOOKING BACK ON BROKEN PROMISES now than she did when she completed it, Dawn answers, "I've learned from every quilt I've done. Sure, I would do some things differently, but that's progress."

About her response to winning this AQS award, Dawn says, "A lot of care and attention to detail goes into each piece I do, along with a lot of personal feeling. It's nice when people appreciate the care and detail and the quilt wins an award, but mostly I hope people share the feeling which was behind the quilt."

"As long as I'm improving, I'm happy. My goal is to take my work as far as I possibly can."

LOOKING BACK
ON BROKEN
PROMISES
53" x 38"
1989
Dawn E. Amos

Joyce Stewart
Rexburg, Idaho

Mountain Memories: How Beautiful Upon The Mountains

"This quilt," says Joyce Stewart, is based on a variation of the Log Cabin and Flying Geese blocks. I call the pattern Double Flying Geese. It is made of half-inch Log Cabin strips with black Flying Geese criss-crossing the blocks." Joyce continues, "I saw a block with Flying Geese going through just one direction and wanted to see if I could do the block with geese going both ways. I thought that idea was original, but before I finished the quilt I had seen two or three with the same pattern in magazines. The color idea just came to me as I worked on the quilt. When I got

second place

*1989 AQS Show & Contest
Wall Quilt, Amateur*

ready to do the last row of blocks around the quilt I decided to change where I placed the darks and lights in the block."

Speaking of the origin of the quilt's title, Joyce says, "I had finished making the blocks and was ready to sew

them together when our parents celebrated their 50th wedding anniversary at my sister's cabin. The whole family all stayed several days, and I suddenly realized that this quilt had all the colors of the mountains in it." Joyce continues, "After I returned home I designed a border for the quilt, and chose to applique wildflowers around the edge, like the pretty wildflowers that we had seen. While in the mountains, my sister and brother-in-law had taken us to a place where there was a whole hillside of glorious ferns, so I also quilted fern leaves around

the border, mixed in with the wildflowers."

Joyce adds, "What inspired this quilt is the hope that people would be able to relate to it and see mountains and trees and streams and wildflowers in it, and that they would be able to enjoy it. I hope that they love the mountains, too, and remember them when looking at the quilt."

Joyce comments on the large number of fabrics – around 100 – she used to capture the colors of the mountains. She says, "Working with lots of different fabrics is one of my favorite things to do. I feel using many different fabrics makes everything blend together beautifully. I loved the quilt when I finished it and even if it had not won I would have still loved it. I do not feel differently about the quilt now, but I do love to share it with others, and when they like the quilt that makes me feel special and really good inside.

To other quiltmakers, Joyce says, "Make only quilts that you are really interested in and that you will want to

"I enjoy my quilts through all the different stages, and when they are done they remind me of things in my life. I really make them for myself, hoping that if they please me, they will also please others."

MOUNTAIN MEMORIES: HOW BEAUTIFUL UPON THE MOUNTAINS
58" x 58"
1989
Joyce Stewart

do your best work on. Try to incorporate your own ideas into your quilts so that they will not be exact copies of other people's work. Entering competitions is good, especially if you want to find out where your strong points and weak points are so that you can capitalize on the strong points and overcome the weak ones by taking more classes or finding out more information about those areas."

Phyllis Howard Soine, Ph.D.
Richmond, Virginia

Pathways Of My Mind

"PATHWAYS OF MY MIND," says Phyllis Howard Soine, "is the second quilt that I made spontaneously, with no pattern. I had only an idea, a sketch with three intersecting lines, and an urge to sew." Phyllis explains how this quilt developed. "After a bad week at work, I came home and started this quilt. My husband called me to the kitchen to eat and I slept a little, but mostly I sewed all weekend. By Sunday night, the top was pieced."

third place

1989 AQS Show & Contest Wall Quilt, Amateur

Phyllis continues, "This quilt expresses how my mind felt. The colors, the balance, the dynamic juxtaposition of the patterns express the contrasts I felt between my wanting to be very orderly and my ending up going different directions. It has excitement and tension, a precarious balance. Even the checkerboards are made of rectangles rather than squares.

"The quilt is constructed of 100% cottons. Several of my quilts incorporate a technique which starts with a background, either strip-pieced or whole-cloth, which I cut apart with my rotary cutter and then put back together in the same spatial relationship but with various strips and segments inserted between the original pieces. This was the first quilt I made utilizing that technique. The quilting lines were marked using a flexi-curve and it was hand quilted. As I marked the quilting, the intersections of the quilting lines started to look like neurons (nerve

cells) with axons and dendrites connecting them, so as I quilted it, I added glass beads to represent the cell's nucleus and nerve impulses traveling along axons and dendrites. I used metallic threads to quilt the 'active pathways.' "

Phyllis's background includes degrees in microbiology, secondary education, and biochemistry from the University of Kansas in Lawrence, KS, and a Ph.D. in toxicology from Virginia Commonwealth University in Richmond, VA. For twenty years she has combined her career in research with her advocation of quiltmaking. She has recently decided to devote herself full-time to quiltmaking.

About this quilt and its award, Phyllis says, "Making this quilt was very exciting, and as time goes by, I become more attached to it. I was surprised but very pleased when it won an award at the AQS show. Although I liked it very much, it was so personal that I did not expect others to appreciate it. The most significant effect winning the

"The most important thing about making quilts is wanting to make quilts. If you want to, you will figure out how to do it. As you make quilts, your skill improves."

PATHWAYS
OF MY MIND
57" x 57"
©1988
Phyllis Howard
Soine, Ph.D.

award had on my life was getting a room at the Executive Inn for the show!"

To other quiltmakers, Phyllis says, "Attending quilt shows enables you to see new ideas, techniques, and fabric and color combinations which stir your imagination and make you WANT to make even more quilts. Seeing other quilts is such an important part of this process, that it is important for quilters to share their work by entering shows. Having a competition associated with the shows adds excitement, encouragement to do your best, and constructive competition for everyone who enters, as well as special rewards for a few. Since my favorite quilts are often not the ones which win the top awards, winning is not as important as exhibiting and sharing."

Caryl Bryer Fallert
Oswego, Illinois

Life In The Margins II: After Autumn

Caryl Bryer Fallert explains, "The overlaid design of this quilt is based on an unconscious 'doodle' of the type that filled the margins of my school notebooks as a child. The background was pieced from 1½" wide strips sewn together in groups of related colors, then cut into equilateral diamonds. The overlaid design was machine embroidered. The quilting was done freehand, and echoes the 'doodle' design of the overlay."

first place

1989 AQS Show & Contest Wall Quilt, Professional

"This is a double-sided quilt," Caryl continues. "The design for the back was based on a variation of the traditional Log Cabin block. It has been altered slightly to make it appear to spiral into the center, echoing the spiral of the overlay design on the front of the quilt. The over-sized block is surrounded by black and white checks, and the 'doodle' design of the machine quilting can be seen more clearly on the back than on the front of the quilt."

After many years of painting, sewing, and experimenting with other media, Caryl discovered that fabric best expresses her personal vision. She loves the tactile qualities of fabric and the unlimited color range possible through hand dyeing. Her award-winning quilts have been included in numerous national and international juried exhibitions.

Speaking of the making of this quilt, Caryl says it was "totally spontaneous and experimental." She elaborates: "I had never made a quilt anything like it before, and I wasn't at all sure then that anyone would like it. It was very gratifying to find out that the judges liked it well enough to give it this wall quilt award."

Asked about her response to quilt shows and competitions, Caryl comments, "Sharing has always been an important part of the quilting tradition in this country. I believe quilt shows provide us with a wonderful opportunity to share our quilts with each other and also with non-quilters. The competition aspect of some shows encourages us to do the best possible work both in design and in craftsmanship."

"My use of a traditional quilt block on the back of the quilt is my tribute to the creative spirits of the anonymous quilt artists of the past."

LIFE IN THE
MARGINS II:
AFTER
AUTUMN
51" x 65"
1989
Caryl Bryer
Fallert

Erika Carter
Bellevue, Washington

Guardians

This original-design quilt by Erika Carter "was inspired by fall's reds, yellows and browns." Erika explains, "I felt the tree trunks would be a challenge in that they created a kind of grid dividing space." Erika has been creating nature-inspired quilts since 1984. She comments, "In my work color, pattern and construction techniques create visual texture."

second place

1989 AQS Show & Contest Wall Quilt, Professional

She continues, explaining her techniques: "Using almost exclusively large-scale prints, I cut the fabric into strips, which I then compose on my felt wall. I machine sew, hand applique and hand quilt all my work. The fragmented nature-inspired imagery expressed in the final composition relates to a personal philosophy based on my own life experiences: life is a textured event and memories, by nature, are but fragments of life."

Speaking of GUARDIANS, Erika adds, "This quilt was my first attempt to portray tree trunks and branches in a stylized manner that suggested some realism. My goal, though, was not realism per se."

Asked about her feelings about this quilt, she says, "I still love the quilt. Though it has sold, the current owner, Sharon Yenter of In The Beginning fabric store, shows it often. It definitely was a turning point in my development of imagery. Since making GUARDIANS, I tend to add more detail than I had before its creation."

Erika adds: "I have really enjoyed the recognition winning an award has provided. Of course, one must have confidence in oneself. After all, that's when the work truly comes from deep within and is really good. But recognition makes me want to work harder, to grow and continue on this rewarding and creative path."

"I believe if the work really reflects what's special about you, the work itself will be special. The effort is in finding how to draw it out and have it come together in a work."

GUARDIANS
55" x 57"
©1988
Erika Carter

Collection of
Sharon Yenter

Bonnie Bucknam Holmstrand
Anchorage, Alaska

Paradise²

Speaking of her background, Bonnie Bucknam Holmstrand says, "I have a long history of playing with fabric. I have been sewing since I was very young and started my first quilt about twenty years ago. It took me five years to finish my first project, but only four days to complete the second. Since then, I have always had several projects in various stages of construction."

third place

1989 AQS Show & Contest
Wall Quilt, Professional

"PARADISE²," says Bonnie, "was done at the request of a friend, Judy Hopkins, who was writing a book on one-of-a-kind quilts. She asked that I make the quilt's focal point a particular size and that I use a certain number of four-inch blocks. No other design requirements were issued. This bird-of-paradise quilt was my answer to her challenge. The focal point of the quilt is an original bird-of-paradise design. The background four-inch blocks were chosen from Judy's 'menu' of simple pieced designs, and the border's leaf design is another original design."

Bonnie explains that the quilt is machine pieced from 100% cottons. The hand quilting includes jungle foliage, bird-of-paradise plants, leaves, and palm fronds. Several colors of quilting thread were used. She adds, "The quilting was designed in sections. One area of quilting was usually completed before the next area was planned."

Speaking of her work,

Photo: G. Craig Freas

Bonnie comments, "My favorite part of quilting is playing with the fabrics and colors and getting all the pieces pinned up on the wall. I seldom do more than a black-and-white line drawing before starting to cut into the fabric. I really enjoy seeing the colors interact and the images come together during that design and construction phase."

Bonnie continues, "Breaking free from the repeat square block was very liberating! I took a workshop from Nancy Halpern in which she said, 'If you can draw it on graph paper, you can piece it.' I took that lesson to heart. Although I still find myself falling back into repeating square blocks, I try to remind myself periodically how many other design possibilities are available."

To other quiltmakers, Bonnie says, "Enter competitions! You have nothing to lose. If you are rejected, you are no worse off than you were when you started. And you may get some constructive comments that help you improve your next quilt."

"Even though in terms of time spent, quilting seems to take a back seat to my other roles as wife, mother, legal assistant, etc., my fiber work plays a very key part in defining my self-image and self-satisfaction."

PARADISE[2]
1989
54" x 65"
©1988
Bonnie
Bucknam
Holmstrand

Collection of
Eugen Karl Holmstrand
Juneau, AK

Charlotte Warr Andersen
Salt Lake City, Utah

She Comes In Colors

"This totally original design," says Charlotte Warr Andersen, "was inspired by a dear friend's love of both the ballet and the rock group, The Rolling Stones. The drawing of the ballet dancer was adapted from a photograph in the book *The Young Ballet Dancer* by Lilliana Corsi."

first place

1989 AQS Show & Contest Pictorial Wall Quilt

The fabrics used were mainly 100% cottons, with a few poly/cotton blends. The figures were hand appliqued; the ribbons and straight lines were machine pieced. A light batting was used and the quilting was done by hand.

Speaking of the development of the quilt, Charlotte says, "SHE COMES IN COLORS was a spontaneous quilt. Most of the quilts I make have months of thought behind them before I ever start drawing. I compose the design thoroughly in my mind. This one began with my finding an appealing picture, and it evolved piece-by-piece as I constructed it. I added here and there, until the quilt told me, 'This is enough. I'm done.' "

About her background, Charlotte says, "I have been making quilts since 1974, professionally since 1983. I make one-of-a-kind, originally designed quilts, and consider myself an artist. Fabric is my chosen medium.

I enjoy entering quilt competitions and have been fairly successful in winning awards, including second place in the first Great American Quilt Festival, and Best of Show, Professional, at the Houston Quilt Festival in 1990."

Charlotte doesn't feel any differently about this quilt now than she did when she made it. She explains, "I loved this project from its conception. It gave me a warm, glowing feeling from the first lines drawn, throughout stitching, even through the tedious act of quilting (quilting is my least favorite part of the process), and on to applying the binding. It's a happy piece and I still smile every time I see it."

Asked about the effect of her award, Charlotte says, "It has added to my reputation, of course. People remember this quilt. Quilters come up to me and say 'oh yes! the ballet dancers! That's one of my all-time favorite quilts.' Of all the quilts I have made so far, it's my favorite, too."

"Do your very best work. Make your quilt to please yourself, not to please the judges. If your heartfelt creativity and love of the work are stitched into the quilt, it will show through to those viewing it."

SHE COMES
IN COLORS
72" x 48"
©1988
Charlotte Warr
Andersen

Elaine Stonebraker
Scottsdale, Arizona

Rising Moons

About this award-winner's design, Elaine Stonebraker explains, "This quilt is completely pieced, using twenty-five or more separate templates." She adds, "All will fit in a rectangle. I maintain some control, but add separate pieces, such as moons, and fit them into the controlled design."

second place

1989 AQS Show & Contest Pictorial Wall Quilt

Elaine continues, "I almost always use 100% cottons. I piece by hand because it is too difficult to piece such small pieces on the machine." She adds, "Quilting by hand is something I enjoy."

Raised in southern California, Elaine attended the University of California at Santa Barbara, majoring in home economics. She has always had an interest in sewing and fabrics. With an airline pilot husband, she has lived in many places in the West, and has spent the last twenty years in Scottsdale, AZ. Eleven years ago she started quiltmaking, quite by accident. She says her first quilt "was made completely by trial and error – mostly error." She has since taken a few classes and attended many workshops. About her development, Elaine says, "My work has evolved from traditional to contemporary style because I do not like the repetition of blocks. I enjoy it when each piece is a decision. That makes work slow, but satisfying."

Elaine comments, "I think pictorial quilts have just

started to receive notice as an art form. I do only pictorial quilts as they seem to be the biggest challenge for me. Since I never pre-draft a design, I was very surprised at the outcome of this quilt. It just developed on its own."

Asked about the effect of this award, Elaine says, "I try a little harder to put my quilts together more carefully. I have always been more interested in the design process, and somewhat weak in the technical part of quiltmaking. The excitement of creating a new pictorial quilt is still my most favorite part, but when I see other quilts that are so perfect, I try a little harder."

To other quiltmakers, Elaine says, "Quite frankly, I truly believe anyone can make a quilt if he/she wants to. I have never had any art or graphic design training; it is all there in the right brain ready to burst forth into an exciting creation that you can be proud of. Make quilts and try to be true to yourself rather than just copy another person's style."

*"RISING MOONS has always been one of my favorite quilts.
I was very surprised when it won an award. I always make my quilts
to please myself, so it is an extra bonus when the judges like them too."*

RISING MOONS
73" x 67"
1988
Elaine
Stonebraker

Museum of AQS Collection

Linda Cantrell
Asheville, North Carolina

The First Thanksgiving

Linda Cantrell explains she started this quilt "when teaching a class that showed students they did not have to know how to draw in order to make pictorial quilts." Linda adds, "Normally I do all my own drawings, but this one was adapted from a greeting card. I was showing students how to modify a design to adapt it for applique."

third place

1989 AQS Show & Contest Pictorial Wall Quilt

Talking about the development, Linda says, "The teepees I tried the first time were too bright, so I took them off and tried new fabric. They were still too bright. I had painted symbols on with fabric paint. I found myself reaching over for the brush, sticking it in the jar and applying 'dirty water' over the tepees. It grayed the color and made it right." Linda adds, "I am not afraid to take the chance of ruining work. Most of my projects involve much trial and error. It may be that I don't have enough respect for my work, but I'm willing to try about anything to make a project successful, even if it might have disastrous effects."

Linda started quilting in about 1981. She says, "Like many, I dabbled in every craft, bought a complete set of books for each and stayed with it for only about two months. When quilting came along, I thought it was just another little whim. Suddenly, I was really at it. I'm addicted now. Every spare minute is taken up with it – teaching, working, designing. I think it's true to say I am a diehard quilt enthusiast."

"Winning the award was wonderful," says Linda. She adds that she thinks it changed the way she views this quilt: "I look at it and think this is better than my others, but I don't think it necessarily is. The ribbon makes me think differently about it."

Linda comments, "I'm very honest with myself. Entering competitions is the only way to go. The first time I entered one, I had no idea what a quilt show was. I put the quilt in and then got the quilt back, with a first place and viewer's awards. But I also received critiques, which highly upset me. I didn't know how they could be critical of an award winner."

Linda continues, "Later I decided that these people knew something. Now I keep all critiques and occasionally go through them to see if there is a pattern, something in my work that many find wrong. I feel my quilts are as good as they are today because I pay attention to these critiques."

Linda suggests to other quiltmakers: "If you listen to critiques and don't just say, 'I did this because I wanted to – I know what I'm doing,' your quilts will be strengthened. We all need to listen. Entering quilt shows has been a very important thing for me. I often wonder if I would make as many quilts if I didn't enter them in shows. Judged shows are a very important part of quilting."

Linda Cantrell says about quilting: "I plan to be doing this for another fifty years!"

THE FIRST
THANKSGIVING
58" x 44"
1988
Linda Cantrell

Diane Roell
Channing, Michigan

Byzantine Mosaic

This quilt is an original pattern developed by Diane Roell. The design, which she describes as having a Middle Eastern influence, was inspired by her fondness for the minaret shape and her interest in Persian rugs.

It took Diane nearly four months to draft the pattern for this intricate design. The quilt is entirely pieced (in all cottons) and quilted by hand – about 2,000 hours were invested in the quilting alone.

Viewer's Choice

1989 AQS Show & Contest

Diane wishes people could see the quilt in person. She explains, "I'd like them to see the quilting on the white areas. It's very close, like stippling – but very organized, with vine patterns, and curlicues, almost feather-like designs. I wanted viewers to look at the quilting and think it was random stippling, and then look more closely and discover the patterns."

Diane continues, "I learned a lot with this quilt.

It is my first original quilt, my first handmade quilt. It almost got away from me. In my design it had another twenty-inch border; I had to eliminate that border and make the quilt a smaller size. I hated to do that because it wasn't the way I'd originally planned it. But I have learned you have to be flexible and change as you go."

Asked if she feels any differently about her quilt now, Diane replies, "I would probably do some things differently. I don't know if there is any project I wouldn't do differently looking back. When I look at it, there are things I think it needs. I still think it needs that extra border. It has too much white in the center."

About her background, Diane says, "At that time I had been quilting for about ten years. I had begun because it was very interesting and because I liked learning about its history. I have always been interested in sewing and needlework. I learned to quilt by myself and began by making projects to give away and soon

started doing commissioned pieces as well."

Diane continues, "I am a registered nurse. Since making this quilt, two of my children have entered college and I am back in college myself, so I have had to go back to work full-time. I have gotten away from quilting, but I intend to go back to it again. I have just had to put it on hold. It's all carefully packed in boxes and waiting for me while I work on an M.A. in nursing."

Asked about the effect of her award, Diane comments: "Recognition is wonderful." She adds that awards have been part of her "life blood."

To other quiltmakers, Diane says, "Make a quilt the way that it is in your heart. You really have to make it the way that pleases you." She adds, "Don't lose faith and give up. Large projects, can become frustrating – they take a long time! When I was doing all the close quilting on this piece, I would turn a light on and crawl under the quilt frame to look at the quilt and its stitching. That kept me going."

*"The quilt was on a huge frame for a long time, rolled up
so that all I could see was the one strip I was working on at the time.
I was petrified that it wouldn't be square. When I finally
took it off the frame, the quilt took my breath away."*

BYZANTINE
MOSAIC
104" x 104"
1989
Diane Roell

Sharon A. Slimmen
Holman, Wisconsin

Tumbling Blocks Star

Sharon A. Slimmen has been sewing clothing since she was 12 years old, and she is now 54. She adds that she is the mother of three sons, stepmother of three girls and two boys, and grandmother of seventeen. Very active, she has done most sewing crafts, ceramics, crochet, macramé, needlepoint, and cross stitch. She has also been involved with

first quilt award

1989 AQS Show & Contest

Arabian horses, training and showing them as a hobby. She adds she enjoys "country living and antiques" and plays golf "for the fresh air and sunshine, not the score."

Speaking of her award-winning quilt, Sharon says the pattern was developed from a quilt made by Mrs. Alvin Waltner of Freeman, SD, featured in the Spring 1984 issue of *Quilt World Omnibook*. The design involved only one template, which "seemed to this beginner a simple enough project."

Sharon adds that the border was her own design.

To make the quilt, she "started with teal and burgundy print in the center star of the blocks and gathered teals and burgundies to use on the natural muslin background." She then "pieced the blocks and center stars and joined them with muslin and teal joining pieces." For the quilting design, she used one-quarter-inch echo quilting in all muslin areas.

Asked about her award, Sharon says, "I didn't think

the quilt was good enough for competition. I did not see the beauty in it until well after I got over being tired of all the work. I now look at it on the guest bed and appreciate it and the talent of all quilters over the years who worked under poor light, with little money and no prize except love from a grateful recipient."

About her award, Sharon says, "It has led to more quilts being made by me, a machine quilting business of my own (regular sewing machine), and some teaching – all in my home. I now know I can do something others may see as pretty, good, and worthwhile. It's nice to have an identity separate from daughter, wife or mother. Those are important titles, but quilter is something I earned on my own."

To other quiltmakers, Sharon says: "Take the plunge! I wasn't going to enter my quilt at all. Do your best and try." To make her point, Sharon adds, "You'll never see your quilt in this book if you haven't made it."

"I encourage people to look at this quilt with both eyes, with one eye, and from different angles, to appreciate the different optical illusions which I was not aware of myself until I saw it hanging at our local show in fall 1988."

TUMBLING
BLOCKS STAR
72" x 90"
1988
Sharon A.
Slimmen

INDEX/QUILTMAKERS

INDEX/QUILTS

~American Quilter's Society~

dedicated to publishing books for today's quilters

The following AQS publications are currently available:

- **Adapting Architectural Details for Quilts,** Carol Wagner, #2282: AQS, 1991, 88 pages, softbound, $12.95
- **American Beauties: Rose & Tulip Quilts,** Gwen Marston & Joe Cunningham, #1907: AQS, 1988, 96 pages, softbound, $14.95
- **America's Pictorial Quilts,** Caron L. Mosey, #1662: AQS, 1985, 112 pages, hardbound, $19.95
- **Applique Designs: My Mother Taught Me to Sew,** Faye Anderson, #2121: AQS, 1990, 80 pages, softbound, $12.95
- **Arkansas Quilts: Arkansas Warmth,** Arkansas Quilter's Guild, Inc., #1908: AQS, 1987, 144 pages, hardbound, $24.95
- **The Art of Hand Applique,** Laura Lee Fritz, #2122: AQS, 1990, 80 pages, softbound, $14.95
- **...Ask Helen More About Quilting Designs,** Helen Squire, #2099: AQS, 1990, 54 pages, 17 x 11, spiral-bound, $14.95
- **Award-Winning Quilts & Their Makers: The Best of AQS Shows – 1985-1987,** edited by Victoria Faoro, #2207: AQS, 1991, 232 pages, soft bound, $19.95
- **Classic Basket Quilts,** Elizabeth Porter & Marianne Fons, #2208: AQS, 1991, 128 pages, softbound, $16.95
- **A Collection of Favorite Quilts,** Judy Florence, #2119 AQS, 1990, 136 pages, softbound, $18.95
- **Dear Helen, Can You Tell Me?...all about quilting designs,** Helen Squire, #1820: AQS, 1987, 56 pages, 17 x 11, spiral-bound, $12.95
- **Dyeing & Overdyeing of Cotton Fabrics,** Judy Mercer Tescher, #2030: AQS, 1990, 54 pages, softbound, $9.95
- **Flavor Quilts for Kids to Make: Complete Instructions for Teaching Children to Dye, Decorate & Sew Quilts,** Jennifer Amor #2356, AQS, 1991, 120 pages., softbound, $12.95
- **Fun & Fancy Machine Quiltmaking,** Lois Smith, #1982: AQS, 1989, 144 pages, softbound, $19.95
- **Gallery of American Quilts: 1849-1988,** #1938: AQS, 1988, 128 pages, softbound, $19.95
- **Gallery of American Quilts 1860-1989: Book II,** #2129: AQS, 1990, 128 pages, softbound, $19.95
- **The Grand Finale: A Quilter's Guide to Finishing Projects,** Linda Denner, #1924: AQS, 1988, 96 pages, softbound, $14.95
- **Heirloom Miniatures,** Tina M. Gravatt, #2097: AQS, 1990, 64 pages, softbound, $9.95
- **Home Study Course in Quiltmaking,** Jeannie M. Spears, #2031: AQS, 1990, 240 pages, softbound, $19.95
- **Infinite Stars,** Gayle Bong, #2283: AQS, 1992, 72 pages, softbound, $12.95
- **The Ins and Outs: Perfecting the Quilting Stitch,** Patricia J. Morris, #2120: AQS, 1990, 96 pages, softbound, $9.95
- **Irish Chain Quilts: A Workbook of Irish Chains & Related Patterns,** Joyce B. Peaden, #1906: AQS, 1988, 96 pages, softbound, $14.95
- **Marbling Fabrics for Quilts: A Guide for Learning & Teaching,** Kathy Fawcett & Carol Shoaf, #2206: AQS, 1991, 72 pages, softbound, $12.95
- **Missouri Heritage Quilts,** Bettina Havig, #1718: AQS, 1986, 104 pages, softbound, $14.95
- **Nancy Crow: Quilts and Influences,** Nancy Crow, #1981: AQS, 1990, 256 pages, hardcover, $29.95
- **No Dragons on My Quilt,** Jean Ray Laury with Ritva Laury & Lizabeth Laury, #2153: AQS, 1990, 52 pages, hardcover, $12.95
- **Oklahoma Heritage Quilts,** Oklahoma Quilt Heritage Project #2032: AQS, 1990, 144 pages, softbound, $19.95
- **Quiltmaker's Guide: Basics & Beyond,** Carol Doak, #2284: AQS, 1992, 208 pages, softbound $19.95
- **Quilts: The Permanent Collection – MAQS,** #2257: AQS, 1991, 100 pages, 10 x 6½, softbound, $9.95
- **Scarlet Ribbons: American Indian Technique for Today's Quilters,** Helen Kelley, #1819: AQS, 1987, 104 pages, softbound, $15.95
- **Sensational Scrap Quilts,** Darra Duffy Williamson, #2357: AQS, 1992, 152 pages, softbound, $24.95
- **Sets & Borders,** Gwen Marston & Joe Cunningham, #1821: AQS, 1987, 104 pages, softbound, $14.95
- **Somewhere in Between: Quilts and Quilters of Illinois,** Rita Barrow Barber, #1790: AQS, 1986, 78 pages, softbound, $14.95
- **Stenciled Quilts for Christmas,** Marie Monteith Sturmer, #2098: AQS, 1990, 104 pages, softbound, $14.95
- **Texas Quilts – Texas Treasures,** Texas Heritage Quilt Society, #1760: AQS, 1986, 160 pages, hardbound, $24.95
- **A Treasury of Quilting Designs,** Linda Goodmon Emery, #2029: AQS, 1990, 80 pages, 14 x 11, spiral-bound, $14.95
- **Wonderful Wearables: A Celebration of Creative Clothing,** Virginia Avery, #2286: AQS, 1991, 168 pages, softbound, $24.95

These books can be found in local bookstores and quilt shops. If you are unable to locate a title in your area, you can order by mail from AQS, P.O. Box 3290, Paducah, KY 42002-3290. Please add $1 for the first book and 40¢ for each additional one to cover postage and handling.